political
correctness
and the
theoretical
struggle

FRANK ELLIS

First published in 2004 by
Maxim Institute
49 Cape Horn Rd, Hillsborough, Auckland
Ph (09) 627 3261 Fax (09) 627 3264
50 Acacia Avenue, Riccarton, Christchurch
Ph (03) 343 1570 Fax (03) 343 0569
www.maxim.org.nz
Copyright © 2004 Frank Ellis

ISBN 0-476-00235-4

Design: Maxim Institute
Printing: Source Design & Print

Endorsements from leading academics

"Frank Ellis has given us a splendid account of the horrible re-emergence of politically correct thinking, or rather mulish refusal to think. He rightly objects not only to the vapidity of the notions put forward, but also to the even more revolting infliction of them on much of the vulnerable public by edict, and he effectively shows the frame of mind as just what nourished Leninist partiinost, with dreadful mental as well as physical results. Closed minds, Ellis shows, mean trouble."
Professor Robert Conquest, Hoover Institution on War, Peace and Revolution, Stanford University, California, author of *The Harvest of Sorrow: Collectivization and the Terror-Famine* (1986) and *The Great Terror: A Reassessment* (1990).

"If asked what I know about "political correctness", I would respond with words and phrases about its American origins, and the pressures spread in universities by senior academics to force a high degree of conformity on colleagues, especially the younger ones, and students, amounting in many cases to enforced ideological conformity leading to a sine qua non, essential to the attainment of higher degrees. Dr Frank Ellis has delved further into its history, tracing it back to Lenin's obsession with ideological conformity and persecution of those reluctant and courageous enough to resist the pressures. In this short work, he offers a stimulating, if controversial, history of his theme."
Brian Crozier, UK, author of *The Rise and Fall of the Soviet Empire* (1999).

"Like "The Cold War", "political correctness" has a history that is much longer than is generally recognised. In this pioneering study, Frank Ellis shows convincingly that "pc" is a Russian Communist invention, going back to the times and plans of Lenin, and an intrinsic part of the unprecedented system of total censorship introduced by the Bolshevik leadership in the late autumn of 1917. Through one of the ironies of history, just when the "Soviet experiment" was beginning to run out of steam after the partial dethroning of Stalin, political correctness took on a new life in the West, where people with a dogmatic mindset utilised (and are still utilising) this concept to try to control and limit the freedom of expression in an attempt to brainwash entire societies in ways that make one wonder whether Lenin has risen from his mausoleum. Ellis's essay is essential reading for everyone who wants to understand the way history is moving at the beginning of the new millennium. This stimulating work should be included in numerous anthologies of path-breaking articles on politics, political philosophy and totalitarianism."
Martin Dewhirst, Honorary Research Fellow, Department of Slavonic Studies, University of Glasgow.

"This remarkable work, as its title indicates, explores the history of the concept of political correctness and then, finding its origin in Lenin's "new conception of party", it proceeds to attend to its applications to justify terror, torture, and man-made famine first by Lenin and his successors in what became the USSR and later by Mao Tse Tung in China. The topical interest of his work lies in the author's demonstration of how, by promoting its ideas of what is and is not politically correct, the New Left throughout the English-speaking world has acquired an inordinate degree of censoring power on university campuses and in the media."

Antony Flew, emeritus professor of philosophy, University of Reading, author of *Crime, Punishment and Disease* **(1973 & 2002),** *Education, Race and Revolution* **(1984) and** *Equality in Liberty and Justice* **(1989).**

"Ellis's trenchant yet scholarly analysis demonstrates that PC is not just a silly fad or a trivial nuisance. By excavating its theoretical roots in communist ideology, the author reveals that PC is a dangerous threat to our freedom and a corrosive force subverting democracy. He is to be congratulated for providing the citizenry with argumentative antidotes to this fashionable nonsense."

Professor David Marsland, Brunel University, London, UK, author of *The Empire Strikes Back: The Creative Subversion of the National Curriculum* **(1993) and** *Welfare or Welfare State?* **(1996)**

"This important study reveals political correctness to be something far more than affected academic jargon or pretentious bureaucratic practice. By demonstrating its origins in the revolutionary political parties that founded the Soviet Union and Communist China, Frank Ellis shows how it embodies a mindset directly at odds with free and independent thought and expression. He reveals how the acceptance of this outlook into contemporary Western society is fostering moral nihilism. The discovery by its adherents that language is an essential lever of power revives one of the central doctrines of totalitarian societies. Political correctness, Ellis demonstrates, is corrupting our cultural institutions, especially the news media and universities, while its devotees are using the state to re-order our thoughts and lives. This profound and scholarly work shows that political correctness is no laughing matter."

Keith Windschuttle, Australian author of *The Killing of History* **(1997 & 2000) and** *The Fabrication of Aboriginal History* **(2002).**

Contents

Foreword

In January of 1989 I was the guest of Novosty Press. For two weeks I travelled between Moscow, Leningrad (as it still was), and the Far East. It was the most fascinating two weeks of my life. Mikhail Gorbachov was overseeing the demise of the great socialist dream but the academics and journalists I interviewed and talked with maintained the party line.

In Vladivostok I lunched in the home of a Professor of Politics. He and his wife, a teacher of English, lived on the third floor of an apartment building designed to look more like a gulag. They were very house proud. Downstairs was covered in graffiti. There was a gap an inch wide between toilet door and frame. I watched them at lunch time while I went, yet my host argued violently that we in the West could never be happy under capitalism.

Other memories include old women sweeping the streets with twig brooms (full employment) and filling the water tanks on the train between Vladivostok and Khabarovsk at 3.00 a.m. in sub-zero temperatures.

Back in Moscow we attended a tiered lecture hall where a mayoral candidate was electioneering. Soon a woman in front of me stood up, shook her fist and shouted at the stage. She was followed by a nearby man. "What", I asked my host, "are they so angry about?"

Instead of talking of Soviet problems far from the Capital, what was he going to do about crime and traffic in Moscow, they wanted to know.

I remember being stunned by this newfound freedom of speech—it was a long way from the times when you could be imprisoned for complaining about hunger if there was no official food shortage declared. Being in Moscow to experience the early transgressions against Party Correctness was a privilege.

It was a privilege also to interview British academic Dr Frank Ellis earlier this year. His ability to articulate the trajectory of political correctness (PC) and its links with the former Soviet Union was a pleasure to hear. His New Zealand meetings were filled to overflowing but his words fell on too few ears.

I first began to mention this new trend about 1990, give or take. Listeners complained. The PC phenomenon was happening in America but many believed it would never catch-on and it could never reach New Zealand. With the passing of a very short space of time, however, it began to affect all developed countries, particularly those in the English speaking world: the US, Britain, Australia, Canada and New Zealand.

What appeared as a ripple has, in more recent years, become a raging torrent. What George Orwell wrote about sixty years ago is now fruit ripening on the tree. We once aimed for equal opportunity; we now demand equal outcome. Unless, of course, race qualifies us for special privileges. And to ensure these things, we are "gifted" with race relations, human rights and equal opportunity commissioners.

As Thomas Sowell wrote, "Social visions differ in their basic conceptions of the nature of man". Start with the wrong concept and the following developments will eventually crumble. That darling of the left, multiculturalism, relies on the belief that all cultures are compatible. They are not. Education based on what you choose to believe will produce ignorance. When your child suggests that factual answer you give is only an opinion, then it's time to change schools. When truth is a variable and science is ruptured by voodoo.

And when history can be rewritten to accommodate the latest "ism", it can't be long before there is no history.

In *Global Warming in a Politically Correct Climate*, M. Mikhel Mathiesen writes that PC, "can easily be mistaken for a conspiracy against reason. A conspiracy, by definition, requires an agreement by many to act toward a single end. No such agreement is evident. Instead we are dealing with a phenomenon which may be better described as a spontaneous collective action; the result of too many of society's components choosing to follow a path of least resistance in the absence of a compelling, commonly shared reason to do otherwise."

With the end of the Cold War, socialism morphed into a range of "isms". It was very successful at assuming new forms and expressions and aligning with "wider causes" such as feminism, the normalisation of same-sex relationships, and so on. PC provides an all-embracing framework to help advance these agendas, and with official state support, continues to gain momentum. Few make the connection with the bloody roots of PC in 20th century Soviet and Chinese communism.

The mere mention of communism and the totalitarian state still has the ability to cause fear in the hearts and minds of most New Zealanders; but talk about PC and many of those same people would simply laugh it off. To suggest any links between PC and Marxism, Leninism, and Maoism will also be met with disbelief. Many of our current left-leaning politicians are "champagne socialists"—they enjoy the trappings, titles and privileges of a structure steeped in tradition, but they simultaneously preach a contemporary form of Marxism seeking to dismantle the received framework of Western civilisation. PC is one of their key tools.

And PC is no laughing matter; we need to read Frank Ellis and see why—indeed, we ignore his message at our own peril.

Leighton Smith
Broadcaster

Introduction

The suddenness with which political correctness entered the public domain in the period between 1989-1991, and the ensuing arguments about the legitimacy of Western culture which lasted until well into the mid 1990s, implies that political correctness is a very recent phenomenon, the origins of which are to be found in certain intellectual trends of the late twentieth century.

Richard Burt, for example, in an essay published in *Censorship: A World Encyclopedia*, argues that the term "political correctness" was first introduced by the New Left in the 1960s.[1] Certainly, thinkers of the New Left developed the concept, but long before Marcuse and Derrida, and a host of other New Left and postmodernist writers were required reading on the campus, we find political correctness established as an ideological criterion of Marxism-Leninism. Official Soviet sources clearly show that the term was in use as early as 1921.[2]

If one takes into account the role of Lenin as the architect of the Soviet Union, and his massive influence in shaping Soviet ideology, then a reasonable assumption is that it is Lenin to whom we must turn in order to find the conceptual origins of political correctness and the term itself. Soviet sources support this assumption.

A review of a diverse and large body of Soviet and Western literature, written and published throughout the twentieth century, which was conducted in preparation for this book, repeatedly identifies the theme of "correctness"—ideological, political or theoretical—as a concern of exceptional importance for Marxism-Leninism and Maoism. The range of sources is impressive: Lenin's own writings before and after the start of the twentieth century; some early resolutions of Communist Party congresses; the insights of writers and philosophers, for example, Joseph Berger, George Orwell, Czesław Miłosz, Stefan Amsterdam-ski, Leszek Kolakowski, Balint Vazsonyi[3], Arthur Koestler and Alain Besançon; the writings of Mao, and other official Chinese sources; victims of Soviet psychiatric abuse; Chinese and Soviet dissidents; scholarly studies, both Soviet and Western, of Soviet propaganda, agitation and media[4]; and the works of some of Russia's greatest writers, most notably, Andrey Platonov, Boris Pasternak, Vasiliy Grossman and Alexander Solzhenitsyn.

> If one takes into account the role of Lenin as the architect of the Soviet Union…it is Lenin to whom we must turn in order to find the conceptual origins of political correctness.

Soviet and Chinese manifestations of political correctness are worlds of paranoid suspicion, endless show trials, false confessions and struggle sessions. They are worlds where the workings of the rational mind are viewed with suspicion, even hatred.

For the hapless victims ensnared in the web of communist ideology it was frequently a matter of life and death, as has been massively documented by Alexander Solzhenitsyn, Robert Conquest, Harry Wu and many others. In the aftermath of the Soviet experiment, Russian scholars have explored the connection between Soviet ideology with its insistence on correctness and the consequences for Russian culture. Their observations leave no doubt that political correctness was an ideological criterion which applied to all spheres of intellectual endeavour.

Having lived under a system where verbal spontaneity and scepticism could sometimes be fatal, and having experienced the party's attempts to police thinking, these former Soviet citizens, and their Chinese counterparts, offer acute insights into the problem of political correctness in the West today.[5] They repay careful study.

Lenin, Partiinost' and Political Correctness

In fashioning an élite revolutionary party, Lenin was obsessed, perhaps tormented, with questions of ideological purity and orthodoxy. Theoretical considerations were paramount: "Without a revolutionary theory", he wrote in *What is to be Done?*, "there can be no revolutionary movement".[6] Only a specifically revolutionary theory, Lenin believed, would prevent the incipient revolutionary movement from abandoning "the correct path".[7]

Despising the exemplar of liberal democracy represented by England[8], Lenin believed that if a small revolutionary party was to maintain its sense of purpose and seize power, then it had to avoid becoming just a forum for discussion, with all the in-fighting and factionalism that involved. Party discipline and the sense of purpose could only be maintained, according to Lenin, if there was a rigidly enforced party line on all questions: from the materialist explanation of knowledge and reality, the supposed crisis of imperialism which led to World War One, to a free press or the role of women in the future communist utopia; there was, if the party theoretician knew his seminal and patristic texts, a politically correct answer.[9]

Lenin himself, as in so many things Soviet, set the precedent and the standard for dealing with deviations from the party line. His tone varies according to the status of the addressee. Lenin can be the teacher, impatient with some sceptic who lacks his commitment to ideology, or, fearing the criticism of his peers, he shows himself to be the master of the *ad hominem* attack.

In an article first published in 1906, in response to a draft resolution of a party congress, demanding freedom to criticise, Lenin accused the resolution's drafters "of totally, incorrectly understanding the relation between *freedom of criticism* within the party and the party's *unity of action*" (emphasis in original).[10] "The Central Committee's resolution", argued Lenin, "is incorrect in essence and *contradicts the party's statutes*" (emphasis in original).[11] Even Plekhanov, one of Russia's foremost interpreters of Marx, was attacked by Lenin for, *inter alia*, "incorrectly assessing the real relationship of the proletariat towards both the government and the bourgeoisie".[12] In his ferocious polemic Lenin asks "whether comrade Plekhanov has "acted correctly" and answers his own question: "No, he has behaved completely incorrectly".[13] In a later article, also published in 1906, Plekhanov came in for another bout of Leninist invective: "He [Plekhanov] is profoundly mistaken. "Treachery" is not "a strong word" but the sole correct expression from a scientific and political point of view to describe the actual facts and the actual aspirations of the bourgeoisie".[14] One can note here, in passing, that Lenin conflates political and scientific correctness in his riposte to Plekhanov. Karl Kautsky, another prominent interpreter of Marx, received the same treatment when in *The Dictatorship of the Proletariat* (1918) he warned of the violence that would ensue from the Bolshevik dictatorship. As a counter attack Lenin wrote *The Proletarian Revolution and the Renegade Kautsky* (1918), consigning Kautsky to the ranks of the ideologically damned. Lenin's manner of dealing with politically incorrect deviations justifies Grossman's observation that: "In an argument Lenin did not seek the truth [*istina*], Lenin sought victory".[15]

To assist his drive for ideological paramountcy Lenin invented *partiinost'*, which in English translation can mean "party membership",

> Lenin was obsessed, perhaps tormented, with questions of ideological purity and orthodoxy.

"party-mindedness" or "party spirit". To this list one could also add "party truth" (see Berger below).

According to Kunitsyn, *partiinost'* was first used by Lenin in 1894 in a dispute with opponents concerning the objective state of knowledge.[16] Knowledge and truth, argued Lenin, are a product of one's class. In fact, what is called objective knowledge is a part of the bourgeois conspiracy to retain power and control so that the working classes can be exploited. In non-Marxist thought truth and knowledge are merely bourgeois biases.

This dispute features prominently in all Marxist-Leninist polemics and adumbrates the intellectual relativism of postmodernism, specifically that truth is a matter of perspective. The idea that knowledge and truth (and latterly perspective) are class-specific (or in Neo-Marxism community-specific) defines the Leninist notion of *partiinost'*, as can be seen from the following:

> If, having examined the origins of this question, one tries to formulate the concept of *partiinost'* which emerges from Leninist assumptions, then it may be looked at in the following manner: the *partiinost'* of ideology (in particular journalism, literature and art and so on) is then *the conscious struggle of the ideologue, theoretician, publicist, artist (of each using his own specific means) for asserting the interest of one or another social class* (emphasis in original).[17]

A later Soviet study reaffirmed the basic thrust of what we are to understand by *partiinost'*:

> *Partiinost'* in communist propaganda is fidelity to the higher class interests of the working class and its mission of the revolutionary transformation of the nature of social relations. The principle of *partiinost'* rejects the pretensions of bourgeois ideology and propaganda to "non-*partiinost'*", "objectivity" and "pluralism" as masking the bourgeois mechanism of social control.[18]

Taking his lead from Lenin, Kunitsyn, in his analysis of *partiinost'*, repeatedly emphasises the correctness of Leninist teachings. Thus, he refers to "the correctness of the chosen path".[19] Various supporters of the Bolsheviks are upbraided for being "unable correctly to understand Bolshevism".[20] Of another party member we are told that he "lost the correct orientation and was even ready to accuse Lenin of "factional tendentiousness"".[21] Certain individuals, who though willing to sacrifice their lives for the cause, "did not always act and think correctly".[22] Colleagues who make ideological mistakes need to be the focus of "correct work"[23] and problems of culture are to be resolved in "a correct Leninist way".[24] Then we are instructed as to the need for "the foundation of the correct relations of the proletariat and the revolutionary intelligentsia".[25]

Even science must submit to the dictates of *partiinost'*: "Lenin's solution of the problem of the interrelationship of gnosiological and political *partiinost'* enables us correctly to understand the problem of the *partiinost'* of science, correctly to set about the practical selection of authors writing in the press on scientific questions".[26] The frequency with which Kunitsyn and other Soviet interpreters of Lenin—and later, Mao—identify Marxist-Leninist orthodoxy with correctness and ideological absolutism reveals much about the state of Soviet scholarship in this field, and elsewhere. We are confronted here not so much with a study of a serious subject but rather a sustained panegyric, even a hagiography, of Lenin, the father of all theoreticians, in which the hagiographers are more concerned to demonstrate their own political correctness than intellectual rigour.

Lenin's concept of *partiinost'* is, I believe, the most likely progenitor of political correctness. For it is *partiinost'* that accounts for the unusual ferocity of all of communism's ideological disputes, whether they are being carried on among various intra-party factions or directed at external enemies. Lenin is quite clear that non-*partiinost'* separated the socialist from the bourgeoisie: "Non-*partiinost'* is a bourgeois idea; *Partiinost'* is a socialist one".[27] *Partiinost'* is the hallmark of ideological purity: non-*partiinost'* identifies the ideologically deviant. Kunitsyn identifies three main types: *revolyutsionnaya partiinost'* (revolutionary party spirit); *kommunisticheskaya partiinost'* (communist party spirit); *politicheskaya partiinost'* (political party spirit).[28] Given the various meanings that can be attributed to *partiinost'*, and the fact that the theory of *partiinost'* was still being ideologically modified in the years before 1917, the mutation of *politicheskaya partiinost'* (political party spirit/truth) into *politicheskaya pravil'nost'* (political correctness), was not an unpredictable outcome. Certainly, there existed a need for such a formulation.

In the Manichean mindset created by Leninism a term was required, which, unlike *partiinost'*, contained an explicit reference to right/wrong, correct/incorrect from a political or ideological point of view, one that could be used to indict those deviating from the party line in an authoritative manner. *Politicheskaya pravil'nost'*, that assertive, impressive sounding and approving criterion of orthodoxy, satisfies this requirement very well indeed. We might see political correctness as a practical solution to a problem arising from the theoretical discussions surrounding *partiinost'*.

Lenin refined his position on *partiinost'* in *What is to be Done?* and the influential article "Party Organisation and Party Literature" (1905). In its revolutionary, communist or political forms *partiinost'* went beyond being merely politically correct, and was elevated to the realm of science (see, for example the response to Plekhanov above). Now, this should not be taken as an appeal to discredited bourgeois notions of objectivity, but should instead be seen as being based on a higher form of rational thinking, that of class consciousness or *soznanie*.

The ideology of class makes possible a new, powerful mechanism for interpreting the world; scientific socialism no less.[29] Science and scientific method, as it had evolved

'Again! Louder!
I can change my spots!'

since Newton, could not escape the need for a correct understanding of the world, one that was congenial to Marxism-Leninism.[30] Where science clashed with Marxist-Leninist ideology, as it frequently did in the course of the twentieth century, then scientists were expected to confess to "errors" and recant, or were arrested. Lysenkoism was one of the better known communist witch hunts against scientists who presented or implied conclusions contrary to Marxist-Leninist orthodoxy.

Liberated from the burden of proof, Lenin and his successors were allowed to claim superior insight. The consequences were profound. By insisting on party unity at all costs and instilling fear of factionalism, Lenin made serious intellectual discussion impossible.[31] Absolute theoretical certainty or, rather, the belief that the party had uncovered the laws of historical progress justified all means necessary to bring about the new society. To quote Valentin Turchin: [...] "society is either structured "correctly" (i.e., in accordance with the laws of Nature) or "incorrectly" (i.e., in contravention of them). In the latter case, society must be ruthlessly destroyed and then rebuilt".[32]

Censorship of all writing is fully justified.

Consistent with the creation of a revolutionary élite to guide the masses, great emphasis in Lenin's writings is attached to ensuring that the right people work in the party press, that they be thoroughly well versed in Leninist thought and that they have an intuitive understanding of what is politically/ideologically correct. *Pravil'nost'* informs all aspects of publishing and the dissemination of ideas, particularly translations of foreign literature which carry a heightened risk of ideological deviation. To this end, notes Kunitsyn, "our party supports among the flood of publications that which helps the correct understanding of life".[33] We are warned that not all authors can be relied on to provide a "correct understanding" of class character[34] and "in the long term", writes Kunitsyn, "the correct education of authors acquired a much bigger role".[35] Lenin, we are also assured, believed that "the workers, confronted with a Marxist explanation of any complicated situation, would correctly understand" and "he [Lenin] showed such boundless punctiliousness in correcting errors which had been made in the party press".[36]

Lenin was also concerned "about the correct implementation of revolutionary principles in the press",[37] and revolutionary struggle and its interests required a "correct, fundamentally scientific reflection of them in the press".[38] In other words, censorship of all writing is fully justified.

This insistence on the link between correct thinking and writing means that journalism and writing become the collective responsibility of the party. It is expressed in one of Lenin's most oft-quoted lines: "The newspaper is not only a collective propagandist and collective agitator, it is also a collective organizer".[39] The paper was intended to educate the masses politically, preparing them under the guidance of the party for the day of revolution. With this end in mind Lenin insisted on "the correct supply" of material for the paper and "on its correct dissemination".[40] As a later official Soviet source makes clear, one of the tasks of party propaganda is "to elucidate for the benefit of the working masses the correctness of the party's policy [*pravil'nost' politiki partii*] and the need to implement it".[41]

Free and open discussion, which existed in the West, represented the greatest threat to Lenin's arrogation of intellectual infallibility. Two points can be noted. First, a free press protected in law cannot be easily manipulated, and Lenin can, of course, be attacked with impunity. Journalists will resist control by a small group of individuals—Lenin's party for example. Second, the very lack of centralised control means that the concentrated essence of ideology, deemed by Lenin to be a precondition for the pursuit and consolidation of power, will not be achieved. This leads to heterodoxy, ideological deviation and debasement of the medium for less serious purposes (entertainment, sensationalism, tabloid journalism, for example). Nevertheless, Lenin argues that within the party: "Free speech and the freedom of the press must be total"[42], subject to the caveat that the party reserves the right to expel those who propagate anti-party views. Regarding the procedure to be adopted for ascertaining "anti-party views", Lenin makes the following point:

The party's programme, the party's tactical resolutions and its code and finally the entire experience of international social-democracy, of international voluntary alliances of the proletariat, which while constantly incorporating into their parties individual elements or trends, which are not entirely consistent, Marxist, or correct, but, additionally, constantly initiating periodic "purges" of their party, shall serve to determine the line separating party views from anti-party ones.[43]

So the party, in order that it preserve orthodoxy, must resort to periodic purges of incorrect elements whose incorrect status shall be determined by the party élite in accordance with the doctrine of democratic centralism. Lenin provides an ideological justification for terror against the party itself and against any opposition to the party from outside. In such apparently innocuous, theoretical beginnings we find the genesis of communist terror which has had truly catastrophic consequences in the twentieth century. Terror itself is politically correct.

Harsh administrative measures to eradicate factionalism from party ranks were stepped up after 1917. Demonstrations of ideological orthodoxy become crucial for survival. Evidence of the party's determination to root out factionalism and other heresies can be seen at the 10th Party Congress in 1921. The resolution "Concerning Syndicalist and Anarchistic Deviation in Our Party" (16th March 1921) is particularly important. Anarchist ideas were singled out and attacked, because in the words of the resolution, they were "fundamentally, theoretically incorrect, representing a complete break with Marxism and Communism...."[44] The formulation of the question concerning the relations between the party and the wider, non-party masses was "incorrect"[45], and the anarchists were also attacked for the "incorrect understanding of the Communist Party's role in its relation to the non-party, working masses".[46] Moreover, attempts by those under fire to cite party documents to support their case were regarded as being "fundamentally incorrect".[47] The real danger to those accused of deviation comes in paragraph five:

Apart from theoretical disloyalty and a fundamentally *incorrect* [*nepravil'nyi*] attitude towards the practical experience initiated by

Soviet power in the field of economic construction, the congress of the RKP, in the views of the aforementioned group and analogous groups and persons, sees *colossal political incorrectness* [*gromadnaya politicheskaya nepravil'nost'*] and an immediate political danger for the preservation of power on behalf of the proletariat (emphasis added).[48]

Returning to ideas first expressed in *How to Begin?*[49], Lenin, in a letter to Kurskii dated 17th May 1922, submitted an amendment to the Soviet Criminal Code. Free of all practical restraints, the theoretical struggle now gives way to physical extermination of class enemies. Terror reaches its politically correct apotheosis:

Despite all the shortcomings of the draft, the fundamental idea is, I hope, clear: that is openly to bring forward a principled and politically correct[50] (and not merely narrowly juridical) statute, which sets out the *essence* and *justification* of terror, its necessity and limits.

The court must not eliminate terror—to promise that would be self-deceit or a trick but is to put it on a sound principled foundation, to legitimise it, clearly, without any lies or evasions. It must be formulated as widely as possible, since only a revolutionary feel for justice and a revolutionary conscience will stipulate the terms of use as widely or as not. (Emphasis in the original).[51]

By the time of Lenin's death in 1924, and certainly no later than the end of the 1920s, the concept of correctness was pervasive in ideology, politics, psychiatry, education, literature, history, jurisprudence, culture and economics. To be politically correct meant to be consistent with, not deviating from, the party line on any given issue.[52] To be politically incorrect was to run the risk of being denounced as engaging in "revisionism", "factionalism", being a "wrecker" or "an enemy of the people".[53] Even the choice of children's names was affected,[54] and a recent study of early Soviet reading habits also shows the astonishing lengths to which the Soviet state was prepared to go to ensure that the correct opinions were formed and internalised by readers.[55] The withdrawal of books published in Tsarist times, as part of a systematic policy of ideological indoctrination, clearly anticipates the contemporary feminist and multicultural approach to education at all levels.

Lenin's death opened the way for Stalin to step up his plotting against his main rival, the flamboyant and intellectually brilliant Trotsky. Accusations of factionalism and deviation from the party line were the main weapons. At the 13th Party Congress held in March 1924, the first after Lenin's death, factionalism was condemned in absolute terms:

> The slightest manifestation of factionalism must be prosecuted in the severest possible manner. The firmness and united stand of the RKP on the basis of the unshakeable principles of Leninism are the most important preconditions of the revolution's future successes.[56]

Exploiting his position within the party bureaucracy, Stalin pursued his ideological vendettas with even greater zeal than Lenin. At a plenary session of the Central Committee in 1925, Trotsky's "anti-Leninist assessment of the role of the peasants" was denounced as "incorrect" and "particularly dangerous" [...] "when the future successes or failures of the revolution are being determined precisely by the correctness or incorrectness in the mutual relations between the proletariat and the peasants".[57] As the founder of the Red Army and a major player in the Civil War, Trotsky was the target of the plenary session's demand that the military leadership be "a model of party discipline and a model of correct understanding of the mutual relations of the proletariat and peasantry".[58]

Having secured Trotsky's expulsion from the party in 1927 and his deportation from the Soviet Union to Turkey in 1929 (and his assassination in 1940), Stalin was now free to concentrate on the ideological and then the physical destruction of Bukharin. Once again, questions concerning the peasantry were the weapons to be deployed. At the Joint Plenum of the Central Committee and the Central Control Commission in 1929, Bukharin was attacked for his "anti-Leninist political line".[59] His views were condemned as being "incompatible with the party's general line".[60] His statement that severe taxation was party policy was "incorrect and false",[61] and the party rejected as "incorrect" any suggestion that it had failed in comparison with the previous year to increase supplies to the countryside.[62] The following, especially the second paragraph, can be regarded as a deadly blow:

> If, despite the existence of all these facts, Bukharin still considers it necessary to blacken the work of the Central Committee and to wage a struggle against its policy in the field of the peasant question, incorrectly asserting that the Central Committee decides one thing, but something different is carried out, then this means that Bukharin does not share the party line, that he is putting forward another line, one that is different from that of the party.
>
> But there cannot be two lines in the party. Either the party's line is incorrect, in which case Bukharin is right [*prav*], so dissociating himself from the Central Committee. Or the party's line is correct in which case Bukharin's "new" line on the peasant question cannot be anything other than a move towards Frumkin's line, which is intended to unleash capitalist elements.[63]

Dissent or deviation was not just politically incorrect but regarded as symptomatic of some profound mental disturbance.

Further, multiple instances of Bukharin's political incorrectness were adduced *ad nauseam*. His assertion that the currency situation was hopeless was rejected as "totally incorrect"[64], as was his assertion that there was no internal party democracy ("totally incorrect and false through and through"[65]). His stance on running *Pravda* was "totally incorrect"[66], and Bukharin's article, "Notes of an Economist" was described as "totally incorrect".[67] And if this was not enough, his overall criticisms were once again rejected in the conclusion as being "totally incorrect criticism".[68] In their ferocity, obsessive nature and ideological prolixity, these attacks adumbrate the same hysteria engendered by Mao against his enemies during the Cultural Revolution. Preselected for extermination, the victims are doomed, no matter what they say or do to defend themselves.

By the late Soviet period dissent or deviation was not just politically incorrect but regarded as symptomatic of some profound mental disturbance. Khrushchev, in a major policy speech to writers, whom, echoing Stalin, he called "engineers of human souls",[69] set the tone:

> Crime is a deviation from the accepted norms of behaviour in society, which is not infrequently caused by confusion in a person's psyche. Can there be illnesses, psychic disorders among individuals in a communist society? Apparently there can be. And if there are, they will be misdemeanours, which are peculiar to people with an abnormal state of mind. So one will not judge a communist society by lunatics such as these. To those, who, on a similar "foundation", might start to call for a fight against communism, one can say that there are indeed people who are fighting against communism, with its noble ideals, but, evidently, such people are manifestly not in a normal state of mind.[70]

Dissent went on to become a factor in determining whether an individual should be incarcerated and is a recurring theme in the well documented abuses of dissidents in Soviet psychiatric institutions in the 1970s and 1980s.[71]

Political Correctness and socialist realism

With its tradition of realism and social criticism, Russian literature had attracted the attention of the party well before 1917. Lenin's essay, "Party Organisation and Party Literature" can rightly be seen as a foretaste of the sort of controls and expectations that would be imposed on journalists and writers. In the one-party state artistic endeavour would not be permitted to exist and function independently of the party. It would serve the ideological goals of the state. Initially, in the years before 1917, Lenin made some effort to appeal to his non-Marxist audience by arguing that writers and journalists who wrote for money were merely slaves of capital, whereas the writer who placed his talent at the disposal of the party was engaged in some noble activity. After 1917, with power seized, the free press banned and the censorship apparatus initiated by decree, the pose of reasonableness could be dropped. Thereafter, authorial freedom was defined purely in terms of a willingness to commit oneself to the party and its goals.[72]

Stalin's rise in the party coincided with a greater prescriptiveness regarding literary policy and led ultimately to the promulgation of the literary doctrine of socialist realism in 1934. Henceforth, art for art's sake was condemned. One of a number of notorious examples of socialist realism is Nikolai Pogodin's *The Aristocrats* (1934), which portrays former thieves and peasants undergoing *perekovka* (reform through labour) while building the White-Sea canal. The reality was something else. Prisoners were not "reformed" through labour at all but merely worked to death in appalling conditions in order to build a canal which, architecturally and practically, was of little value. A recent study, in which the author applies a postmodernist approach to the history of the canal, does to the memory of the victims what Soviet propaganda did as well: denies their suffering by relativizing and burying it under spurious theories. The author argues that: "Pogodin acted politically correctly, in contemporary parlance, and was rewarded for it with success and publication".[73] In both the context of the 1930s and that of the 1990s one could say that Pogodin acted "politically correctly".

Socialist realism demanded that artists depict the world as it ought to be, not as it was. Again, this principle has been thoroughly grasped by feminists and appears to be the holy of holies among practitioners in our contemporary broadcast and print media. It is, too, as any interested American parent can confirm, crucial in the production and marketing of contemporary school textbooks, many abandoning any pretence of historical accuracy in the name of "balance" and "fairness". Likewise, affirmative action and equal opportunities programmes and legislation are predicated on a theoretical template that owes little to empirical data and human behaviour.

An important point here, and one that explains a great deal about Marxism-Leninism and Neo-Marxism, is the distinction made in Russian between *pravda* (truth which is socially, morally or ethically just) and *istina* (the truth, the empirical state of affairs, that which nature makes possible or impossible). For the Marxist-Leninist, and more recently the multiculturalist and feminist, empirical reality (*istina*) is the enemy, since the Soviet ideologue and his current imitators are pursuing a socially and morally higher truth (*pravda*). This somewhat arcane difference between the two types of truth in Russian was thoroughly understood by the former communist, Joseph Berger:

[*Istina*] denotes the correspondence between the notion and the objective reality. *Pravda* is a unique and specifically Russian concept: it means the highest concept of truth, a truth elevated to the rank of an idea. It is etymologically linked with *pravo* ["right" or "law"] and with *pravosudie* ["process of justice"]. A Russian who "stands for *pravda*" or who "struggles for *pravda*", does not stand or struggle for the sum of all kinds of truth, big and small, but for the truth which needs to be attained, truth in action, the ideal of conduct, the correspondence between acts and the demands of ethics. Perhaps in English one would have to say "the right truth" or "knowledge plus righteousness", but this splits the concept—and in the thirties this split created an abyss. In the rooms of the NKVD [Soviet secret police] and at Party meetings, *istina* was nothing—it was relative and it could easily be changed: only *pravda* was absolute. It seemed to me, as it must do to millions of others who have not been through this school, hard to understand how a philological distinction could have such an effect on the lives of so many. But in fact this small difference—this tyranny of *pravda* over *istina*—was the lever by which white was turned into black; no such dialectic had existed since the Inquisition. The notion of *pravda* was the basis of power.[74]

Berger illuminates not just the deadly split in Soviet ideological thinking but, equally, the intellectual schizophrenia, the intellectual and moral relativism and the dishonesty that characterises so much of the multicultural agenda. His use of "the right truth" is, in essence, what feminists and postmodernists wish us to understand by the term politically correct. Biological differences between men and women—an insignificant *istina* as far as feminists are concerned—must not be permitted to undermine the struggle for *pravda*, the great truth, in this case, the absolute equality of condition between men and women and the absolute equality of all outcomes.[75]

Czesław Miłosz has written at length on the excruciating moral and intellectual damage done to Polish writers who, accustomed to writing before the imposition of Soviet rule, now had to adapt to socialist realism. Of one colleague who fell foul of the new method,

Milosz writes that 'a politically correct theme would not have saved him from the critics' attack had they wanted to apply orthodox criteria, because he had described the concentration camp as he personally had seen it, not as one was *supposed* to see it' (emphasis in the original).[76] To the insights of Berger and Milosz in this area can be added those of Arthur Koestler (*Darkness at Noon*, 1940), George Orwell (*1984*, 1949) and Alain Besançon, (*The Falsification of the Good: Soloviev and Orwell*, 1994).

One writer of exceptional importance for this theme in twentieth-century Russian literature is Andrei Platonov whose novel, *The Foundation Pit* (1929-1930), is a study of alienation brought on by the ideological corruption of language. As the slogans, bureaucratese, jargon and a never-ending flood of acronyms overwhelm the language, Platonov's characters lose the ability to communicate with one another. Crushed by the weight of ideology (and anticipating the distinction made by Berger between *istina* and *pravda*), one character ponders whether "truth [*istina*] is a class enemy".[77]

Words there are aplenty in this politically correct cacophony but their meaning has been appropriated by the party. Language is a series of ideological rituals. Denied the means to express their hopes and fears, Platonov's characters regress to a state of fearful isolation. Silence becomes the only effective form of communication. Corrupting language, communism destroys community, the very thing that communists purport to be creating. Well before Orwell, Berger and Miłosz, Platonov identified and satirised the attempt made by the party to change reality by a conscious policy of making certain words and ideas redundant, or politically incorrect, and replacing them with appropriate or politically correct ones.

In both manifestations—that depicted in Platonov's novels, or that favoured by postmodernists—the intention is to use language as a weapon. In this scenario language is not primarily used to communicate ideas but rather to signal the speaker's willingness to submit to the politically correct register ("gay", for example, in place of "homosexual", or "gender" in place of "sex"). Language is power not for the masses but for the party intellectuals who are to instruct us on correct usage. Contemporary political correctness pursues the same policy by dominating public discourse and creating a climate of fear such that "incorrect" opinion is declared "illegitimate", "extreme" or "racist" and so on.

The Sino-Soviet schism,
Mao and the cultural revolution

Correct thinking in Chinese communism owes much to Mao's political personality and ambitions and, as in the case of Lenin in the Soviet variant, arose in part from the need to impose a general line on the party cadres and the population as the party attempted to modernise the country.

Factors peculiar to China would be the role of face and the legacy of Confucianism. From Confucianism comes the custom in Chinese culture whereby disciples of some revered master, in the first instance Confucius, would collect the master's sayings (*yü-lu*) for posterity. [78] *The Quotations from Chairman Mao Tse-Tung* (*Mao chu-hsi yü-lu*) have been put together with the Confucian tradition in mind.

The Soviet precedent also helps to explain why Mao wanted to launch the Great Proletarian Cultural Revolution.[79] In *Dr Zhivago*, one of Pasternak's characters, looking back at the 1930s, argues that collectivisation was such a calamity that the party could not acknowledge it and so in order to hide the failure all means were used to force people to lose the habit of independent thought and judgement.[80] Precisely the same problem confronted Mao after his policies caused a massive famine which in terms of human suffering, misery and the numbers of dead, has no parallel in human history. Objective reality, that is, the deaths of tens of millions by starvation, had to be forced from people's minds by terror. So the stage was set for this great and ancient nation to descend into self-inflicted madness goaded on by Mao and his teenage thugs. The masses, that category of amorphous, docile worker ants so beloved of Marxist theorists everywhere, had to be kept in a state of permanent frenzy and suicidal enthusiasm. Acting, not thinking, was the requirement of the time.[81] Scepticism was a heresy, and so by one of those paradoxes in which communism abounds, correct thinking meant, in essence, not thinking at all.

Jing Lin's study of the political, psychological and educational factors which prepared the Red Guards for the violence they inflicted on their fellow Chinese during the "ten-year calamity" (*shinian haojie*), as the cultural revolution is now referred to, confirms the extreme emphasis on all types of correct behaviour and thought in Maoism. Communist ideology was sacrosanct, "the only correct official ideology".[82] As in the case of its Soviet counterpart, the Chinese mass media's main task was to indoctrinate the masses with "correct attitudes, ideas and beliefs".[83] And the main task of the highly centralised education system was to inculcate "the correct political orientation".[84]

We are dealing here with a fanatical faith which is impervious to reasoned argument and evidence, not so much thought but "anti-thought".

Another parallel with Soviet Russia (and National Socialist Germany) was the party propaganda machine's use of young role models specifically aimed at the Red Guards (see, for example, Pavlik Morozov in the Soviet Union and Horst Wessel in Nazi Germany). The Chinese exemplar was Lei Feng, a young communist whose diary inspired the "learn-from-Lei-Feng movement' in which the Red Guards would keep diaries and hand them in to teachers "for help in correcting possible deviations".[85] Attitudes among the Red Guards were comparable to those identified by Berger regarding *istina/pravda*: "While being absolutely obedient to Mao and aggressive against the "class enemies", the Red Guards treated the proletariat as embodying a concept of "justice", and an idea that represented correctness".[86]

Extracts from *Important Documents on the Great Proletarian Cultural Revolution*, which was published in 1970 at the peak of the cultural revolution, as well as those from other official Chinese sources, confirm Lin's conclusions and, again, the absolutely central role of correctness in all fields of Maoist thought and Chinese communism.[87] If anything, centrality understates the emphasis. We are dealing here with a fanatical faith which is impervious to reasoned argument and evidence, not so much thought but "anti-thought". The following citations—and many more could be cited—require no explanation. They demonstrate an even greater obsession with correctness than that found in Lenin and his interpreters:

[...] "our Party will always forge ahead victoriously along the correct course charted by Chairman Mao";[88]

"Under the guidance of Chairman Mao's correct line" [...];[89]

[...] "the great, glorious and correct Party;"[90]

"Long live the great, glorious and correct Communist Party of China!";[91]

[...] "the correct kind of leadership";[92]

"Without correct literary and art criticism it is impossible for creative work to flourish";[93]

"China is a great socialist state of the dictatorship of the proletariat and has a population of 700 million. It needs a unifying thought, revolutionary thought, correct thought. That is Mao Tse-tung Thought. Only with this thought can we maintain vigorous revolutionary drive and keep firmly to the correct political orientation";[94]

"Red Guard fighters, revolutionary students, the general orientation of your struggle has always been correct";[95]

[...] "the correct line of Chairman Mao and the bankruptcy of the bourgeois reactionary line";[96]

"Only by thoroughly criticizing and repudiating the bourgeois reactionary line and eradicating its influence can the line of Chairman Mao be carried out correctly, completely and thoroughly";[97]

teachers are to understand the "correct line" of Chairman Mao;[98]

"Not to have a correct political orientation is like not having a soul";[99]

"Mao Tse-Tung's thought is the life-line of our Party, the sole correct supreme guiding thought of our Party, also the sole correct supreme guiding thought of the international communist movement";[100]

"Incorrect expressions must be eliminated from newspapers and journals".[101]

Political correctness in Chinese communist ideology must also be interpreted against the background of the Sino-Soviet split. Chinese communists found it unforgivable that Khrushchev could denounce Stalin and promulgate a doctrine of peaceful coexistence with the West which implied either a suspension of, or a retreat from, the class struggle. Scandalised by such ideological revisionism—though this did not prevent China from welcoming President Nixon in 1972—the Chinese communist party saw itself as the one true bastion of ideological purity. Khrushchev was a dire warning of where incorrect thinking would lead. Extreme ideological vigilance was needed if China was not to lapse into revisionism as well.

Some sense of what Soviet revisionism meant for communist China can be understood in the Communique of the 11th Plenary Session of the Chinese Communist Party 8th Central Committee (August 12th 1966).

According to the communiqué "the CPSU [Communist Party of the Soviet Union] has betrayed Marxism-Leninism, betrayed the great Lenin, betrayed the road to the great October Revolution, betrayed proletarian internationalism, betrayed the cause of the international proletariat and of the oppressed peoples and oppressed nations, and betrayed the interests of the great Soviet people and the people of the socialist countries".[102] So concerned was the Chinese Communist Party leadership with the Soviet line that in the 1960s it established an Anti-Revisionist Writing Team whose specific task was "to compose authoritative denunciations of Soviet-style "revisionism" in the name of the CCP Central Committee".[103]

Internal dissenters, or those deemed to be traitors and revisionists, were subjected to brutal treatment by the state media—literally trial-by-media—especially where the victim was a high profile member of the party. Thus, in a report of the Chinese Communist Party's Central

Committee, Liu Shao-Chi, who had disagreed with Mao, was referred to as a "renegade", "traitor" and "scab".[104] Lesser figures would be attacked at a local level and those deemed to be guilty of serious deviations from the party line could face the dreadful pressure of a struggle session in which they were subjected to prolonged physical and psychological abuse, often in front of large audiences, and were called upon to repent their crimes. Other methods were rectification campaigns designed to correct "bad thoughts", and a variation on the struggle session known as unity-criticism-unity, which involved breaking the victim down, "deconstructing" him, as it were, and then putting him back together again.[105]

Worse still was the thought reform, *si xiang gai zao*, that was practised in the Chinese concentration camp system, the *laogai*, or "Auschwitz of the mind" in Harry Wu's startling expression.[106] "For the Chinese communist", notes Wu, "the aim is not to destroy him [the prisoner], a hostile element, physically through violence, but to destroy him mentally and ideologically, while threatening him with violence".[107] Certain forms of physical abuse are used in conjunction with thought reform, as in the degrading ritual of *bai lao men* ("paying respects to the cell god"), which involved a new prisoner being made to suck up excrement from a bucket through straws and then saying that the excrement tasted delicious.[108]

Compelling prisoners to act out their roles, in what to the Westerner, appears to be the theatre of the absurd, plays a major role in breaking the prisoner's mental resistance. The more grotesquely at odds with the truth, the more blatant the distortion and accusation, the more powerful the intellectual violence done to the victim. Agreeing to some blatant fabrication, the victim damages and eventually destroys his ability to think for himself, which is consistent with the Maoist view that: "'Self'" is the origin of all evil".[109] His inner self destroyed or broken, the victim ceases, finally, to be an independent, thinking human being.

Political Correctness
and the New Left

Mao's Great Leap Forward inspired and encouraged a new generation of "political pilgrims" to suspend their critical faculties in much the same way that an earlier generation of Western communists and fellow travellers had embraced Stalinism.[110] Mao's cultural revolution also provided a convenient backdrop to the Vietnam war protest and the wave of student rebellion and resentment directed at white middle-class society.

The New Left itself was a product of the 1960s. Its message was simple: "All power in the world is oppressive, and all power is usurped. Abolish that power and we achieve justice and liberation together".[111] "Impatient for doctrine"[112], this was a generation ripe for the teachings of Lenin and Mao, and much in Althusser, Derrida, Foucault, Gramsci, Galbraith and Marcuse. Yet, for all the pose of rebellion, the break with the existing order and hierarchy, this was a movement that craved submission to authority; the more hostile the New Left was to bourgeois mores and behaviour and the more outrageous its claims, the more tightly it controlled the minds of its youthful followers.

Louis Althusser can lay claim to being the master sorcerer of the New Left whose manipulation of language entices the unwary, leading to intellectual confusion and oblivion. From Michel Foucault the radical derives his obligatory paranoia and the belief that the boundary between the deviant and the natural is a monstrous bourgeois fiction designed to perpetuate bourgeois rule (an echo here perhaps of Lenin on the free press). Jacques Derrida teaches him the need to deconstruct language and literature which prepares the way for attacking the canon of Western literature (the hegemonic discourse of the white, heterosexual ruling class).

Antonio Gramsci stressed the importance of revolutionary theory: "Gramsci did for the sixties what Lenin and Stalin had done for the thirties and forties: he convinced his following that revolutionary practice and theoretical correctness are identical concerns" [...].[113] And, while attacking the economic practices of the West, the author of *The Affluent Society* comments that: "In the communist countries, stability of ideas and social purpose is achieved by formal adherence to an officially proclaimed doctrine. *Deviation is stigmatised as "incorrect"*. In our society, a similar stability is enforced far more informally by the conventional wisdom" (emphasis added).[114]

> In the communist countries, stability of ideas and social purpose is achieved by formal adherence to an officially proclaimed doctrine. *Deviation is stigmatised as "incorrect"*.

Galbraith's concluding sentence is a precise example of the intellectual relativism that did so much to create and to perpetuate the view that Western societies and the Soviet Union were one and the same, even indeed, that they were converging (whereupon the Soviet Union in a fit of curmudgeonly ingratitude towards its Western friends and fellow travellers collapsed).[115]

Herbert Marcuse was probably the most influential of all the New Left thinkers. His manipulation of language—one better known example being "repressive tolerance"—continues the assault on empirical reality pioneered by Lenin.[116]

These thinkers and others have contributed in varying ways to what is probably the striking feature of the New Left, and one that sets it apart from conventional Marxism[117]: the extraordinary emphasis placed on culture and language; the belief that language is the essential lever of power. Mao, whose influence was by no means confined to mainland China, has, one suspects, been hugely influential in this respect. To quote H.C. Chuang:

> Ever since the Communists came to power nineteen years ago, every political campaign in China has been simultaneously a semantic campaign as well, introducing or reviving a plethora of shibboleths and slogans with such determination and concentration that it sometimes borders on verbomania or graphomania. Mao strikes one as a true believer of word-magic...[118]

"Word magic" explains why the contemporary notion of political correctness exerts such a beguiling influence on so many discrete groups and factions. For, if money is power, then some will have more power than others. If, however, language is power, then anyone can partake of

power, and groups and factions who otherwise might have very little to say to one another, now find that they are united in their desire to impose new linguistic norms on mainstream bourgeois society which, it is alleged, has traditionally marginalised them.

This new alliance, or rainbow coalition, has a ready ally in the universities, print and broadcast media and public sector bureaucracies. The universities, in particular, are uniquely placed to be the new brokers of language and culture, since it has been New Left ideology ensconced in our universities and on its fringes that has turned the world into language.[119] The universities are crucial to what I call the New Censorship Paradigm (NCP). Despite all the talk of democratising language and social inclusion, the NCP is something that was "constructed" by a small group of intellectuals for their own ends; essentially power over the means of expression. No longer the guardians of our cultural heritage, they actively seek to "deconstruct" it. As I have explained elsewhere:

> Blacks and women now feel that they have the moral authority to impose cultural and linguistic change, that is, "the correct orientation."

This class—or community as it is often called—now regards language—its customs, rituals and use and the culture it creates—as its private domain over which it shall exercise sole dominion. The rest of us have no absolute right to use the language in the same way as used by our mothers and fathers. Rather, we must wait to be invited to participate in public debate on any issue of substance, subject to the approval of the new logocracy. In a curious reversal of the Marxism which used to be the home of many of these people, the new logocracy regards language and culture as its private property. In any disputes its judgement shall be final. Thus we have moved from the struggle to control the means of production, the characteristic of class war and traditional Marxism, to the struggle to control and to regulate the means of expression. Language is the new means of production. The politically-correct intellectual class are its new managers. This is Marxism without the economics.[120]

Instructed by New Left theoreticians that they are victims, that language is power and, better still, that it has been "constructed" to serve the hegemony of the white heterosexual male, blacks and women now feel that they have the moral authority to impose cultural and linguistic change, that is, "the correct orientation". For the "repressed" and their allies this is an intoxicating message. Instead of resistance, they have all too often found a willingness on the part of mainstream culture to submit to their linguistic and relativist demands. Concessions of any kind earn no good will at all. On the contrary, they tend to confirm the radical in his contempt for the society around him, reinforcing his suspicion that society was rotten all along (why else do they make concessions?) and encouraging him to make ever greater demands for institutional and cultural change.

'Smack me on the bottom and you're finished!'

Comparative summary

The main features which Western political correctness derives from its Soviet and Maoist variants can now be summarised as follows:

(i) No limits to the competence of politicians and activists to remould human societies are recognised. There is no area of human cultural endeavour which cannot be "deconstructed" and improved;

(ii) Political correctness denies objective truth, or something close to it. See the *istina/pravda* split identified and discussed by Berger. Robert Conquest, discussing the NKVD's drive to secure confessions during the Stalinist Terror, notes something that is readily applicable to today's commissars of multiculturalism [...] "a determination to break the idea of truth, to impose on everyone the acceptance of official falsehood";[121]

(iii) Only certain types of art, literature, scientific research and thinking are permissible. Soviet ideologues believed, mistakenly, that they could co-opt the tradition of nineteenth century Russian literature for their own ends. Rather than acknowledging the grandeur of the great canon, postmodernists have chosen to attack the canon with the aim of destruction through levelling. Both Western and Soviet/Maoist versions accept the need for truth and facts to be censored if this conflicts with politically correct aims. When Harvard professor, Barbara Johnson, as part of the AWARE campaign (Actively Working Against Racism and

Ethnocentrism), declared that "professors should have less freedom of expression than writers and artists, because professors are supposed to be creating a better world"[122], she reveals her full commitment to the spirit of Soviet socialist realism and Leninist *partiinost'*.

Whereas the Soviet communist party was brutal in regard to censoring forbidden manuscripts, killing and imprisoning writers without hesitation, more diverse approaches are favoured in the West. The following can be noted:

- outright suppression of manuscripts by a publisher, even when the author has been earlier informed that publication will proceed (as in the case of Chris Brand's book on the *g* factor);
- intimidation of publishers by left-wing extremists who often adopt a guise of "anti-racism" or "anti-fascism"; failure or refusal on the part of university librarians to consider certain titles for collection development (a very effective long-term form of censorship);
- refusal to review certain books; ignoring a book even when it sells well;
- organising a discussion panel to attack an author or publication, ensuring that the author

Enormous psychological pressure is brought to bear on academics and students to submit to the general line…

under attack or advocate of certain views has minimal time to respond. This is a favourite technique of the British Broadcasting Corporation, Britain's state-owned television station, when a politically incorrect opinion or book cannot be ignored since to do so merely draws attention to the silence of the state media;

- ideological and political attacks on the institution of free speech, frequently based on the straw man fallacy that free speech is not an absolute (no man-made institution is);

(iv) Use of the print and broadcast media to vilify and to demonise those who break any taboos prescribed in paragraph iii. This is important in the Western version since the totalitarian violence used by the Soviet Union is not currently an option;

(v) We find exceptional importance attached to the need to establish and to maintain correct theoretical approaches. For contemporary political correctness domination of discourse—symbols, words and usage—is all important;

(vi) The role of a demon figure either the class enemy or currently the white, heterosexual male;

(vii) Political correctness has, to paraphrase Thom, turned the world into language. And strives for absolute control over the dictionary;

(viii) Envy is exploited to an unusual degree;

(ix) Freedoms guaranteed in Western societies are exploited in an attempt to destroy those freedoms while arguing that these freedoms are a sham (free speech, equality before the law, freedom of assembly);

(x) The Soviet and Chinese Communist Parties seized power and proceeded on the basis of the *tabula rasa* or Year Zero. In the West we are experiencing a process of slow and incremental Sovietization.

AS SOON AS EVERYBODY CHOOSES THE WRONG SIDE,

IT THEN, BY SOME MIRACLE, BECOMES THE RIGHT SIDE.

Left-liberal responses to criticism of the PC agenda

Emerging into the wider public domain at the end of the 1980s and early 1990s, the term political correctness, much to the surprise and chagrin of those who used it, rapidly became associated with the Pharisee and the tyrant.

As early as 1992, the compilers of *The Official Politically Correct Dictionary & Handbook* were quick to spot the danger and tried to blunt the attack, warning their readers that: "The term 'politically correct', co-opted by the white power elite as a tool for attacking multiculturalism, is no longer 'politically correct'".[123] Attacking political correctness with some vigour in *Culture of Complaint*, Robert Hughes nevertheless felt obliged to balance his criticisms with the invention of "patriotic correctness", which, he assured us, was as bad as political correctness.[124]

Richard Burt's explanation of the origins of political correctness as something that was "used ironically against other leftists as a critique of moralism and preachiness"[125] also shows a certain lack of imagination and understanding of what is at stake. For, if political correctness was simply a question of ridiculing "preachiness" or adopting poses then one could just ignore it.

On the basis of the material cited and discussed here, political correctness goes way beyond mere finger-wagging. In its Maoist variant, it represents an extreme form of intellectual violence designed to break an individual's will and compel him to submit to the will of the collective (community). Harry Wu's insight into his own ordeal in the *laogai* recognises the brutal simplicity of what his tormentors were trying to achieve:

> Suddenly the traditional practice of footbinding came to mind. We have switched to headbinding, I thought. It's no longer the fashion to bind a woman's feet, but they bind a person's thoughts instead. That way the mind can't move freely. That way ideas all take on the same size and shape, and thinking becomes impossible. That's why they arrested me. That's why they want to change me, that's why they force me to reform.[126]

Western versions lack concentration camps for re-education and reform through labour, yet they indisputably involve wholly unacceptable levels of censorship and intellectual violence to those who dissent from multicultural orthodoxy. Race awareness courses in American universities are just one example.[127]

Moreover, the threat and use of physical violence is always there if the left feels that some recalcitrant academic needs to be taught a lesson. Orchestrated mob rule which was used to intimidate professors Michael Levin, J. Phillipe Rushton, Chris Brand, Arthur Jensen and Hans Eysenck, is straight out of the Maoist canon of street thuggery deployed against Chinese intellectuals during the cultural revolution. Burt's citing others to the effect that no academics have been prevented from teaching or dismissed by any university administration is disingenuous, and demonstrably wrong.

In the United Kingdom, Ray Honeyford, the headmaster of a school in Bradford—an inner-city area with a large concentration of schoolchildren from the Indian sub-continent—was subjected to a sustained campaign of physical violence and bureaucratic intimidation because he highlighted the failures of multicultural education. Some twenty years later he has been thoroughly vindicated, as some of his erstwhile critics and the government now admit.[128] Yet this is small comfort to a decent man whose career was destroyed in its prime. The most recent example was the death of Pim Fortuyn, a former Dutch university professor, who was murdered by left-wing extremists because of his outspoken attacks on the level of legal and illegal immigration into Holland.

Furthermore, anyone who has taught at an American university can testify that enormous psychological pressure is brought to bear on academics and students to submit to the general line on all issues dealing with multiculturalism, race and feminism. The atmosphere is not one which is conducive to asking awkward questions. It is one of coercion. As Robert Lifton has noted in his pioneering study of thought reform: "The message of coercion is: you *must* change and become what we tell you to become—or else. The threat embodied in the "or else" may be anything from death to social ostracism, any form of physical or emotional pain" (emphasis in original).[129]

Nor, given the way tenure is awarded in American universities, are we likely to encounter many dismissal cases. Any academic who publicly or privately dissented on issues relating to multiculturalism would be placing his chances of securing tenure in grave jeopardy. Dissent would lead to negative reviews in the tenure process, the result being denial of tenure, an administrative pre-emptive strike, in effect *de facto* dismissal. Most academics, even with tenure, prefer to stay silent. In the strict sense of the term the question of dismissal does not therefore arise.

Marxism-Leninism, from which all political correctness is derived, manifests a completely different order of correctness and application from any other political system.

That said, attempts have been made to get university administrations to fire tenured faculty for expressing politically incorrect opinions.[130] So far these attempts appear to have failed but they have caused a great deal of stress to the victims and resulted in much emotional and intellectual energy being wasted. In view of the legal security that tenure affords in American and Canadian universities, one is tempted to conclude that university administrations that attempt to fire faculty, do so not in the hope that they will succeed—though that would be a desirable outcome—but rather with the express intention of causing the victims as much misery as possible. If true, and one suspects that this would be difficult to prove in a court of law, then it amounts to a university administration's abandoning the presumption of innocence, a vital feature of Western jurisprudence. The mere fact of your criticising multiculturalism renders you "guilty" and liable to punishment.

Nor were the debates over political correctness in the early 1990s something peripheral to the future of higher education, as Burt has also suggested, but something fundamental.[131] Whatever cause the left-wing radical supports in the rainbow coalition—and these days he need not be very left or very radical—his relativist approach to knowledge, his commitment to the "truth that ought to be" rather than the one that is, his barely concealed loathing of individual excellence, the belief that in the collective or community resides superior wisdom, his loathing of free speech (which he, naturally, exploits to the full) and his ready acceptance of a completely politicised education system, are demonstrably the offspring of communist systems. Political correctness provides the deep structure, the base on which the superstructure

I ACTUALLY PREFERRED THE OTHER COLOUR, BUT WITH ALL THIS POLITICAL CORRECTNESS I DIDN'T KNOW HOW TO SAY SO!

of multiculturalism *et al* can be raised. Political correctness, in other words, is something serious.

Some of Burt's points have been taken up by Helena Kennedy, a well known left-wing Scottish lawyer and supporter of things multicultural and feminist. As recently as May 2002, she restated views made in the mid-1990s, namely that: "Political correctness is an invention of the right".[132] There is plenty of evidence, as I have tried to demonstrate in this book, that by the time the Soviet Union collapsed in 1991, and in any case well before the vast majority of Westerners, whatever their political allegiances, had heard of it, political correctness was established as an indispensable element in the theoretical struggle of Marxism-Leninism, Maoism and the New Left. Correctness after all, (that is the "correct" analysis of Western, bourgeois societies and the "correct" solutions to their ills), has always been the basis on which the Left, new or old, has staked its claim to order our lives and rebuild our societies in the name of "social justice".[133]

Kennedy's assertion therefore, was made either out of ignorance or, more probably, because she understands only too well that the demonstrable and verifiable debt owed by multiculturalism and feminism to Lenin and Mao does nothing to make the public congenial towards the whole multicultural experiment and its oppressive legislation.

Responses other than direct denial can also be noted. The frequency with which we encounter terms such as "correct orientation", "correctness", as well as the use of the adjective and adverb "correct" and "correctly" in official Chinese sources underlines the extraordinary efforts made by the Chinese communist party to control people's thoughts and feelings. Yet the studies consulted for this article betray a marked reluctance to draw conclusions about the communist origins of political correctness and the manner in which it has migrated to the West. Not a single work, cited here, and which was published after 1990, (that is at the time when the debate over political correctness in the West was raging), has actually discussed the connection between Maoist notions of correctness and the American campus, even if only to deny or to attack any connection. With the exception of Jing Lin and Michael Schoenhals[134]—Lin leaving us in no doubt about the importance of correct thinking in the ideological preparation of the Red Guards—Lipman and Farrell[135] and Saunders[136] have tended to avoid using "correct" and "correctness" in their discussion of the ideological pressures applied to Chinese during "the ten year calamity".

Where references to "correctness" *are* made, as in Chung *et al*[137], then the authors conspicuously refrain from making any connection with the West.[138] Only Dewhirst comes close to making a connection in a brief footnote.[139] Chung herself in the introduction clearly identifies the problem of political/ideological correctness in communism yet studiously avoids making any parallels with its contemporary use by Western leftists. However, she does permit herself a parallel with China's past as in "Confucian correctness".[140] Now it is somewhat odd that she can make a parallel with a sage who lived five centuries before the birth of Christ yet not make the more obvious and immediate one with the 1990s. "Confucian correctness" misleads in the same way that "patriotic correctness" does, since it implies that one form of "correctness", be it "Confucian", "patriotic" or "political" is no better or worse than any other. This is the relativism of political correctness itself at work here. To blur these distinctions is to destroy them, or to weaken them to the extent that one can argue, as Galbraith does, that Western "conventional wisdom" and communist political correctness are the same thing. If we proceed from this leftist assumption, then we could argue that there is no "connection" to be made since both systems are not separated but constitute one giant politicised whole.

On this basis not to highlight the evolution of Soviet political correctness, via Maoism to the West's universities and from there to other institutions, is not to ignore the problem, for there is no problem to be ignored. Political systems and empires from Rome to American democracy, the leftist tells us, have always imposed conformity and insisted on correct behaviour. True enough. And what of conservatives, do they not tell us that liberty and "right reason" go together?[141] Why, then, asks the leftist, should communism and the left be singled out for opprobrium? The answer is that Marxism-Leninism, from which political correctness is derived, manifests a completely different order of correctness and application from any other political system. The danger arises from the totalitarian aspirations of Marxism-Leninism-Maoism. All human existence is politicised and everything is judged according to political/ideological criteria and corrected or destroyed accordingly. If a man's mind cannot be "rectified" or freed from "incorrect" thoughts then he ceases to be a man.[142] He becomes an "enemy of the people". Extermination is justified, demanded in fact by the logic and ideology of class war, as is absolutely clear from the abominations of the Gulag and the *laogai*.

The role of ideology—Marxism-Leninism—is crucial, as has been fully explained by Solzhenitsyn:

> Macbeth's self-justifications were feeble—and his conscience devoured him. Yes even Iago was a little lamb too. The imagination and the spiritual strength of Shakespeare's evildoers stopped short at a dozen corpses. Because they had no ideology. Ideology—that is what gives evildoing its long-sought justification and gives the evildoer the necessary steadfastness and determination. That is the social theory which helps to make his acts seem good instead of bad in his own and others' eyes, so that he won't hear reproaches and curses but will receive praise and honours.[143]

Another anomaly is that none of the works consulted includes any references to political correctness in the indexes. This squeamishness to explicitly highlight the connection is perhaps an indirect acknowledgement that political correctness on the American campus and elsewhere does indeed owe a great deal to Mao and his antecedents. It is perhaps born of the fear that any discussion of the connection will provide ammunition for conservative opponents of multiculturalism. Whatever the reason, the lack of any discussion at a time when arguments over political correctness were taking place in the US and Britain, and when some of the authors were working on books about communist China's cultural revolution, is highly unusual to say the least.[144] In the Russian context, the same is true of Ruder and Tolstaya.

PC in Britain

B ritish society suffers from the standard problems generated by political correctness that currently afflict the USA, Canada, Australia and New Zealand: oppressive equal opportunities legislation; the scientifically illiterate assertions of feminism; the cult of "gender"; the absolutisms of multiculturalism; and the attacks on objective truth. Of special interest and importance in Britain are the high profile role of the BBC as an aggressive promoter of political correctness and the effects of *The Macpherson Report* on policing.[145]

Funded by a license fee and thus largely immune from the threat of business failure that hangs over commercial television, the BBC is uniquely able to propagandise a politically correct agenda and, equally, to vilify or to ignore critics. In domestic and international news items, interviews, documentaries, soap operas and films the politically correct agenda is pervasive, relentlessly pushed, and largely unchallenged. In domestic news it is taken for granted that blacks and Asians are always the victims of racism, never the perpetrators. Black failure in education is the fault of white society. Disproportionately high levels of black crime are hardly ever discussed, or if they are hinted at, then, once again, white society is somehow to blame, never blacks themselves.

BBC programmes portray disproportionately large numbers of black and Asian newsreaders, actors and interviewers which serve to create a false impression of their numbers and status in the general population (the BBC's version of socialist realism). In international news items, hostility to America is obligatory, and there is a marked reluctance to show sub-Saharan Africa as anything other than the victim of heartless and rapacious multinationals or cruel Western indifference. That after decades of independence from colonial rule Africans could be responsible for their own misery is never seriously contemplated. The West is always to blame.

A more recent method adopted by the BBC and the left to counter accusations of political correctness, and one more effective than Helena Kennedy's crude denials, is to treat political correctness with a certain disdain or even silence without actually denying its left-wing credentials, and without renouncing the methods and goals of political correctness and multiculturalism. The BBC is especially adept at this sort of Orwellian deceit, appearing to state one thing but encouraging behaviour and attitudes which are entirely consistent with politically correct objectives even if not referred to as such. One favoured ploy is to avoid any use of "incorrect" and go for close synonyms, for example, "inappropriate", "unacceptable" or the very common, "offensive".

> When assertion constitutes proof we have lost our freedoms for good.

Many Russians, Poles, Czechs, Bulgarians and East Germans who revered the BBC as a surrogate domestic broadcasting service during the Cold War will balk at such apparently harsh comments. Yet when it comes to the ugly side of multiculturalism in Britain today, and much of it is very ugly indeed, the BBC lacks that commitment to objectivity and truth, which once made it so feared by the men in the Kremlin. When Greg Dyke, who is appropriately known as the BBC's Director-General, can apologise for the fact that the BBC is "hideously white"[146], one realises the degree to which politically correct ideas now control and shape the BBC. To paraphrase one of its first Director-Generals, the BBC has become a social menace of the first magnitude.

Even BBC staff are now starting to question what is happening. In a recent article, published in the London *Spectator*, Rod Liddle, a former editor of *Today*, the BBC's main current affairs radio programme, accused the BBC of being corrupted by "institutionalised political correctness".[147] This, he argued, was particularly evident in the television coverage of the May 2003 local council elections. The Conservatives, to everyone's surprise, did much better than expected. Moreover, the British National Party (BNP), the only party in Britain that has consistently attacked the scandalously high levels of legal and illegal immigration, won eleven seats, an astonishing achievement in such a hostile media climate, even more so when its leader, Mr Nick Griffin and his party colleagues are subjected to something close to a media blackout. BBC journalists, argued Liddle, were unable to cope with these realities, preferring instead to ignore them because they were simply too threatening to the politically correct worldview inculcated by BBC directives and the compulsory seminars and workshops.

Unfortunately, the "institutionalised political correctness" of which Liddle complains has left its mark on him as well. Castigating BBC censorship of BNP success in the elections, Liddle nevertheless could not resist calling the it "a racist party", the BBC's standard line. This, he argued, was common knowledge: "Even the most disadvantaged, jelly-headed, white, trailer-trash cretin in Burnley knows that the BNP is a racist party", he wrote.[148] Would Liddle write of "black trailer-trash cretins"? Of course not, but disadvantaged whites can be called "white trailer-trash cretins" with impunity. Between Greg Dyke's ingratiating assertion that the BBC is "hideously white" and Liddle's sneering there is no difference. In his desperation to demonstrate his anti-racist credentials, Liddle inadvertently reveals not just his own double standards and those of the BBC milieu that created him and Dyke, but the vicious anti-white racism that pervades the BBC from top to bottom.

Policing in Britain has proved to be extremely vulnerable to the attentions of the politically correct fanatics and ill-informed meddlers, as can be seen from the publication of *The Macpherson Report* in 1999. In 1997 retired judge Sir William Macpherson was asked by the Labour Government to conduct an inquiry into the manner in which the London police had investigated the murder of a black teenager, Stephen Lawrence. The police, Macpherson concluded, had not pursued the murder investigation with sufficient vigour. This, he maintained, was largely due to a culture of "institutional racism".

A disturbing feature of the inquiry and the subsequent publication of the report itself was the hysteria that gripped the left-wing press, the BBC and even some conservative politicians. Worse still was the failure of the police—there were some exceptions—to fight back in the face of this systematic and organised vilification, particularly senior officers. Here, for example, are the thoughts of John Grieve, director of the Metropolitan Police's Racial Task Force, on *The Macpherson Report*:

> I am a racist. I must be because Sir William Macpherson of Cluny said that I am; the Home Secretary said that I am; countless members of the public at the Stephen Lawrence inquiry hearings said that I am; and I have found inside myself evidence of subtle prejudice, preconception and indirect discrimination. It is for others to decide about their own racism. I am for change inside myself and in the behaviour of myself and others.

'You booked a table in our smoking area?'

> The Metropolitan Police Service (MPS) is an institutionally racist organisation. It must be because Sir William said that it is; the Home Secretary said that it is; and countless members of the public at the inquiry hearings said that it is.[149]

Since when has mere assertion alone ever been enough to determine a person's guilt? Law-abiding citizens who expect the police to remain detached from, and to reject, political interference and the ideological hatreds of multicultural extremists should be deeply alarmed by Grieve's self-incriminating hyperbole. (For argument's sake we shall assume it to be genuine rather than an attempt to curry favour with his political masters). Police officers in charge of investigating serious crimes must retain the power of independent thinking, the ability to assess evidence for themselves. They must resist pressure for conclusions that contradict what the evidence suggests. Failure to do so can lead to serious miscarriages of justice. Grieve shows no signs at all that he has retained the power of independent thought. Quite the reverse, Macpherson, the Home Secretary and the mob said he was a racist, *ergo* he must be.

This is the same twisted logic of class war: if Mao's Red Guards say you are an "enemy of the people", you are one. When assertion constitutes proof we have lost our freedoms for good. Grieve has unconditionally submitted to the politically correct agendas of the police haters. In this respect, he follows his master, Sir William Macpherson, who uncritically accepted the Marxist ranting and anti-white racism of black activist, Stokely Carmichael, and the definition of institutional racism provided, without any sense of embarrassment or double standard, by the partisan Metropolitan Police Service Black Police Association.[150]

Another sinister consequence of *The Macpherson Report* was the introduction of something known as integrity testing. Typically, this would mean a black officer's taking a seat next to a white officer in, say, the police canteen and engaging him in conversation in the hope that the white officer would say something "racist" or indeed anything that could be construed as such.[151] Bear in mind that the definition of a racist incident recommended by Macpherson— "is any incident which is perceived to be racist by the victim or any other person"—has been adopted, and one can appreciate just how easy it is to start accusing police officers of racism and, correspondingly, how difficult it is to defend oneself in this atmosphere of Maoist intimidation.

The consequences of *The Macpherson Report* on operational policing, especially in London but throughout Britain, soon became apparent.[152] Fearing accusations of racism, the police avoided black suspects. Levels of violent street crime soared. The pernicious effects of Macpherson's recommendations on rank-and-file police officers and on British society generally can be appreciated in a candid reader's letter published in *The Daily Telegraph* in 1999. The reader and his wife were mugged by three blacks and severely beaten. In his letter, Mr Aspinall noted:

> The policemen to whom I made my statement the morning after were affable and sympathetic but demoralised. The muggers were black, and when I asked the police what percentage of violent crime in London was Afro-Caribbean, they winced and looked at each other but gave no answer.[153]

The reaction of these police officers to a straightforward question highlights the fear of acknowledging and articulating truths deemed by some to be "offensive" or "inappropriate", or politically incorrect.[154] There is no doubt at all that *The Macpherson Report* was a remarkable triumph for the liberal-left, a platform from which to condemn and to humiliate the hated police and British society at large. Senior police officers' publicly accepting unfounded assertions of their guilt shows just how much progress has been made in demoralising an important institution in a civilized society.

Two recent examples complete the picture of moral and intellectual panic and cowardice that dominates any discussion of multiculturalism in Britain. During the 2001 General Election campaign, the Conservative Member of Parliament for East Yorkshire, John Townend, made some outspoken attacks on multiculturalism at a constituency meeting. His views were widely reported and William Hague, the then Conservative Party leader—in a nice demonstration of Leninist democratic centralism that now grips the Tory party—threatened him with immediate expulsion from the party if he did not withdraw his remarks. This Townend duly did with indecent haste. Now he was not standing for reelection and his remarks obviously struck a chord with large numbers of people who did not approve of

'Haven't you got a womenu?'

the multicultural agenda. Yet he capitulated, very publicly. Likewise, Pat Bottrill, head of the Royal College of Nursing's governing council, noted after she had reconvened a meeting that a number of those present at its opening had not returned. This, she quipped, was like the plot of Agatha Christie's novel, *Ten Little Niggers*. Bottrill duly grovelled and resigned.[155]

How much longer, one wonders, before *The Nigger of the Narcissus* (1897), one of Joseph Conrad's masterpieces, will be quietly removed from our libraries and burned in secret?

The alarming aspect in all the cases cited—by no means rare—is not so much the politically correct intimidation itself, though ugly and ubiquitous, but the willingness of the victims to concede that they have in fact done or said something abominable, and then to collude with their attackers instead of standing their ground. Fear of letting slip a politically incorrect remark in communist China, where the consequences could lead to the *laogai* or execution, is understandable, but not in Britain.

Conclusion

Despite the determined efforts of liberals and left-wingers to counter the association of political correctness with their favoured causes, the perception remains among the public that political correctness is essentially a creation of the left. The historical evidence, some of which I have marshalled here, supports that association, though even now few seem to realise just how strong the Soviet legacy is. Enriched by his successors—Soviet, Maoist, feminist, postmodernist and most recently multiculturalist—political correctness still bears the stamp of Lenin, the founder of twentieth-century totalitarianism. The empire Lenin helped to build is, thankfully, no more. Yet one hundred years after his tract in revolutionary subversion, *What is to be Done?*, was first published, his ideas still command a great deal of loyalty. Ideas do indeed have consequences, as Richard Weaver has argued. Contemporary versions of political correctness are Lenin's revenge.

What is it about political correctness that inspires such fear among people in free and open societies? Indeed, can societies in which people are subjected to such psychological pressure to conform to the articles of multiculturalism and feminism—the coercion of "or else", already noted—really be said to be open and free? Have we not lost something? More importantly, can we get it back? Having come this far, I feel obliged to examine, albeit briefly, the question of why so many intelligent people capitulate to the intellectual and moral coercion of political correctness. There are, I think, two reasons.

First, the bureaucracies which we associate with politically correct themes and orthodoxies can only exist because of the surplus capital created by Western economies. By funding these bureaucracies, which are essentially parasitic and contribute nothing to the common weal, we allow the West's superior wealth to be turned against it. Our prosperity has created an enemy within and continues to nurture it. Nor do we just extend millions of tax dollars and pounds. Too many of us have given these politically correct bureaucracies a moral and ethical loan without demanding anything in return.

Second, we must consider the nature of our secular societies: loss of religious faith creates a vacuum. In the absence of God, man must, perforce, fall back on himself. True, man has always thought it would be rather nice to be free of the Decalogue, but he soon finds his new found freedom from God, his essential loneliness, even more intolerable.

By denying or abandoning God, man denies himself the moral and spiritual strength to resist the intrusive demands of the collective, the party, the supposedly superior wisdom of the group. The balance between individual and state tilts dangerously in favour of the latter. The state or party becomes the final arbiter of all moral and intellectual questions. This is overwhelmingly the case in the totalitarian state. It was Trotsky who conceded that: "None of us desires or is able to dispute the will of the Party. Clearly, the Party is always right...We can only be right with and by the Party, for history has provided no other way of being in the right".[156]

In the absence of God and conscience the party becomes the supreme court of our conscience. In a short novel published in 1993, Vladimir Makanin examines the effect of the party tribunal on Soviet life, and casts light, I believe, on something which bedevils Western societies today:

Perhaps the mechanisms by which these inquisitions induce the sense of guilt lie deep in the psyche of the person under investigation. Somehow, the more conclusively the judgement of heaven has been mocked and undermined in Russia, the more these earthly tribunals have sprung up and come into their own. They not only abrogate the judgement of heaven, they appropriate its unbounded competence to their own ends.[157]

On a lesser scale Western societies are confronted with the same problem.

Largely unchallenged, politically-correct bureaucracies have appointed themselves as the moral and intellectual tribunals in our own secular societies. The gradual loss of any religious conviction—especially strong in the feminised Anglican church—erosion which is accompanied by the inevitable growth of moral and intellectual relativism has undermined our confidence in our ability as individuals to make moral and intellectual judgements. In fact, to make such judgements is the new sin. Note what has happened here: the politically correct commissariat condemns us for being "judgemental", yet reserves the right to pass judgement on us.

Collective pressures magnified many times by the ubiquity and reach of the print and broadcast media can very quickly create a climate of fear which most of us, not surprisingly, find intolerable. So we apologise. We withdraw our remarks. We may even resign or be threatened with expulsion from the party to which we have devoted the best part of our lives. Suddenly we discover that we are very much alone and material possessions, those superficial manifestations of individualism, are not enough. In an earlier age we might have turned to God. Now all we know is the world of Caesar. Chastised and bullied in this manner, abandoned by colleagues who we thought had some moral fibre, we fall silent. And this silence in the face of intimidation, which masquerades as the defender of tolerance, is deeply threatening to democratic society.

To conclude I offer two allegories. The first is pessimistic and belongs to the genre of low-budget horror films. Imagine a giant arachnid, defeated and mortally wounded, which in its death throes, manages to ejaculate a stream of spores. The victor, savouring his hard won triumph, fails to see that the spores have landed on his body. If not decontaminated they will begin the process of his metamorphosis into the very monster he has just vanquished.

The second allegory is apocryphal yet optimistic. It instructs us that reality has a habit of fighting back. British troops stationed on the Falkland Islands decided that the island's resident males bore more than a passing resemblance to Benny (a rather dull-witted character in the British soap opera, *Crossroads*). After a while the locals, who doubtless enjoyed watching *Crossroads*, found out that the garrison referred to them as "Bennys". Somewhat annoyed, they complained to the senior British officer. An order was duly issued that henceforth all ranks of the garrison were to cease to refer to the islanders as Bennys, since it was deeply offensive. Some time afterwards a junior officer noted that his men had started to refer to the islanders as "stills". Asked why he called the locals "stills", one of his men replied: "Well sir, they're still Bennys".

Endnotes

[1.] Richard Burt, 'Political Correctness', in Derek Jones, ed., *Censorship: A World Encyclopedia*, Vol. 3, Fitzroy Dearborn Publishers, London, 2001, p1901. In a review of Aidan Rankin's *The Politics of the Forked Tongue - Authoritarian Liberalism* (2002), Charlotte Horsfield cites a US Secretary of State's being the first person to use the term political correctness in 1948. *The Salisbury Review*, Vol. 21, No. 3, Spring 2003, p53. No source is provided by the reviewer.

[2.] *Resheniya partii i pravitel'stva po khozyaystvennym voprosam* (*Decisions of the Party and Government on Economic Questions*) Vol. 1, 1917-1928, Izdatel'stvo politicheskoy literatury, Moscow, 1967, p205.

[3.] Balint Vazsonyi, a refugee from communist persecution, states that his first encounter with the term politically correct was when he read the works of Anton Makarenko, Lenin's expert on education. See Balint Vazsonyi, *America's 30 Years War: Who Is Winning?*, Regnery Publishing Inc., Washington D.C., 1998, p13.

[4.] In her pioneering study of the Soviet media published in 1973, that is well before the term political correctness acquired wide usage, Gayle Durham Hollander made the following observation: "The teacher is a third source of political influence: as a representative of society's authority, she is both an adult model of behaviour, and the perpetrator *of a learning culture in which political correctness is an integral part of scholarly success.* [...] Alternative views of politics are ridiculed or ignored, and Marxism-Leninism is presented as the basis of all knowledge - social, political, aesthetic, and scientific." See Gayle Durham Hollander, *Soviet Political Indoctrination: Developments in Mass Media Since Stalin*, Praeger Publishers, New York and London, 1973, p13 (emphasis added). Note in this respect the Soviet ditty: "if you are ideologically consistent, then you are politically literate."

5. Tat'yana Tolstaya's essay identifies the various themes of political correctness in the West—racism, sexism, lookism—yet understates or largely ignores the repressive legal and intellectual infrastructure that supports political correctness and the corrupting effects on the university, though the Soviet maxim cited by her points to precisely that: "if you don't know then we'll teach you, if you don't want to know then we'll force you". See Tat'yana Tolstaya, 'Politicheskaya korrektnost'' ('Political Correctness'), *Sestry*, Podkova, Moscow, 1998, p131. She also fails to identify the Leninist contribution. Her use of *korrektnost'*, which is a literal translation of the English, instead of *pravil'nost'* is misleading since it implies non-Soviet origins. *Korrektnost'* translates as "politeness", "tactfulness" or "consideration". The same error can be found in *The Concise Oxford Russian Dictionary* Revised edition, Oxford University Press, Oxford, 1998, in which political correctness is translated as *politicheskaya korrektnost'*, p816.

6. V. I. Lenin, *Chto delat'?* (*What is to be Done?*, 1902), *Sochineniya*, Vol. 5, 4th edition, OGIZ, Moscow, 1946, p341. The section from which this is taken is entitled 'Engels concerning the significance of the theoretical struggle'.

7. Lenin, *Sochineniya*, Vol. 5, p341. As David Apter has pointed out: "Lenin, the ideologue of Marxism, reinforced his polemics with claims to superior wisdom. From analysis of 'material conditions', the ideologue can lay down a 'correct' political line for the public to follow. Superior wisdom is equated with ideological authority by means of which the public is converted to the political line. Indeed, ideological purity becomes the rock against which waves of deviationism must be dashed unless they submerge the promontories of revolution." See David Apter, *Ideology and Discontent*, The Free Press, New York and London, 1964, p19.

8. The full force of Lenin's contempt for liberal democracy can be seen in the following response to Kautsky: "Just take the basic laws of modern states, just take the way they run themselves, just take their freedom of assembly or the freedom of the press, take their 'the equality of citizens before the law'—and at every stage you will see the hypocrisy of bourgeois democracy with which every honest and politically aware worker is familiar." See Lenin, 'Proletarskaya revolyutsiya i renegat Kautskii' ('The Proletarian Revolution and the Renegade Kautsky', 1918), *Sochineniya*, Vol. 28, 4th edition, OGIZ, Moscow, 1950, p224. Very little separates Lenin's hatred of liberal democracy from that of today's multiculturalists. Lenin, one suspects, would be very pleased at the way equal opportunities legislation in the USA has subverted the principle of equality before the law.

9. To quote Solzhenitsyn: "Only those who saw the Party's needs in correct perspective could hold their places and march at his [Lenin's] side". Alexander Solzhenitsyn, *August 1914 The Red Wheel 1: A Narrative in Discrete Periods of Time*, trans., H. T. Willets, Penguin, 1990, p168.

[10.] Lenin, 'Svoboda kritiki i edinstvo deystvii', ('Freedom of Criticism and Unity of Action', 1906), *Sochineniya*, Vol. 10, 4th edition, OGIZ, Moscow, 1947, p408.

[11.] Lenin, *Sochineniya*, Vol. 10, p409. Lenin goes on to make the fundamental connection between ideological and political correctness and the Leninist principle of democratic centralism: "The principle of democratic centralism and the autonomy of local branches signifies precisely the complete *freedom of criticism*, covering all areas, provided the unity of *action decided upon* is not violated in the process—as well as the inadmissibility of *any* criticism, which undermines or complicates the unity of a course of action decided by the party." (Emphasis in the original, p409.) In other words, local party branches are free to argue any case only within the framework set by Lenin.

[12.] Lenin, 'Plokhie sovety' ('Bad Advice', 1906), *Sochineniya,* Vol. 10, 4th edition, OGIZ, Moscow, 1947, p412.

[13.] Lenin, *Sochineniya*, Vol. 10, p412.

[14.] Lenin, 'Kak rassuzhdaet t. Plekhanov o taktike sotsial-demokratii' ('How Comrade Plekhanov thinks concerning the tactics of Social Democracy', 1906), *Sochineniya*, Vol. 10, 4th edition, OGIZ, Moscow, 1947, pp437-438.

[15.] Vasilii Grossman, *Vse Techet* (*Everything Flows*), 2nd edition, Possev-Verlag, Frankfurt/Main, Germany, 1974, p169.

[16.] Georgii Kunitsyn, *V. I. Lenin o partiinosti i svobode pechati* (*V. I. Lenin on Party Spirit and the Freedom of the Press*) Izdatel'stvo politicheskoy literatury, Moscow, 1971, p45.

[17.] Kunitsyn, 1971, pp55-56.

[18.] Spartak I. Beglov, *Vneshnepoliticheskaya propaganda: Ocherk teorii i praktiki* (*Foreign Policy Propaganda: An Essay in Theory and Practice*), Vneshnyaya shkola, Moscow, 1984, p362.

[19.] Kunitsyn, 1971, p81.

[20.] Kunitsyn, 1971, p99.

[21.] Kunitsyn, 1971, p163.

[22.] Kunitsyn, 1971, p166.

[23.] Kunitsyn, 1971, p180.

[24.] Kunitsyn, 1971, p183.

[25.] Kunitsyn, 1971, p224.

[26.] Kunitsyn, 1971, p134.

[27.] Lenin, 'Sotsialisticheskaya partiya i bespartiinaya revolyutsionnost'' ('The Socialist Party and the Revolutionary Ethos of the Non-Party Faction', 1905), *Sochineniya*, Vol. 10, 4th edition, OGIZ, Moscow, 1947, p61.

[28.] Kunitsyn, 1971, p80 & p126.

[29.] In an article first published in 1906, Lenin congratulates himself on the "correctness" ("*pravil'nost'*") of dividing the main bourgeois parties into three main types. Lenin, 'Kadety, trudoviki, i rabochaya partiya' ('The Kadets, the workers and the workers' party', 1906), *Sochineniya*, Vol. 10, 4th edition, OGIZ, Moscow, 1947, p420.

[30.] As Françoise Thom has pointed out: "The phrase 'the correctness of Leninist theses' implies that the proposition 'Leninist theses are correct' is true." See Françoise Thom, *Newspeak: The Language of Soviet Communism*, trans., Ken Connolly, The Claridge Press, London, 1989, p83.

[31.] The Chinese communist party proved to be as equally obsessed with eliminating factionalism as Lenin. Note the following: "Within the Party, no action is permissible which violates the Party's political line or organizational principles, nor is it permissible to carry on splitting or factional activities, to act independently of the Party, or to place the individual above the collective body of the Party." See *Documents of Chinese Communist Party Central Committee Sept. 1956 - Apr. 1969*, Vol. 1, Union Research Institute, Kowloon, Hong Kong, 1971, pp5-6.

[32.] Valentin Turchin, *The Inertia of Fear and the Scientific Worldview*, trans., Guy Daniels, Martin Robertson & Company Ltd, Oxford, 1981, p164.

[33.] Kunitsyn, 1971, p100. Under conditions of Maoism, as Michael Schoenhals points out, the problem is especially fraught with dangers for Chinese translators of Western books: "Translators and others professionally engaged in the systematic introduction of foreign thought in China have always been in a precarious situation when it comes to formulations." See Michael Schoenhals, *Doing Things with Words in Chinese Politics*, Chinese Research Monograph Series, Institute of East Asian Studies, University of California, Berkeley, 1992, p117.

[34.] Kunitsyn, 1971, p131.

[35.] Kunitsyn, 1971, p232.

[36.] Kunitsyn, 1971, p160.

[37.] Kunitsyn, 1971, p194.

[38.] Kunitsyn, 1971, p191.

[39.] Lenin, 'S chego nachat'?' ('How to Begin?', 1901), *Sochineniya*, Vol. 5, 4th edition, OGIZ, Moscow, 1946, p10. To quote Angus Roxburgh: "A Soviet propagandist sees himself purely as an ideologist, much more concerned with "correctness' and questions of organisation." See *Pravda: Inside the Soviet News Machine*, Victor Gollancz Ltd, London, 1987, p101.

[40.] Lenin, *Sochineniya*, Vol. 5, p11.

[41.] *Malaya Sovetskaya Entsiklopediya* (*The Small Soviet Encyclopedia*), Vol. 7, 3rd edn., Gosudarstvennoe nauchnoe izdatel'stvo, Moscow, 1959, column 628. One example of the use of *pravil'nyy*, given in Ozhegov's Russian-language dictionary, is *pravil'naya politika* ("the correct policy"). See *Slovar' russkogo yazyka* (*Dictionary of the Russian Language*), 18th edition,

Russkii yazyk, Moscow, 1987, p498.

42. Lenin, 'Partiynaya organisatsiya i partiynaya literatura' ('Party Organisation and Party Literature', 1905) *Sochineniya*, Vol. 10, 4th edition, OGIZ, Moscow, 1947, p29.

43. Lenin, *Sochineniya*, Vol. 10, p29.

44. *Resheniya*, 1967, p204.

45. *Resheniya*, 1967, p204.

46. *Resheniya*, 1967, p204.

47. *Resheniya*, 1967, p204.

48. *Resheniya*, 1967, p205.

49. "From a point of principle we have never renounced and cannot renounce the use of terror." Lenin, *Sochineniya*, Vol. 5, p7.

50. Richard Pipes translates the Russian original—*politicheski pravdivoe*—as politically correct. See *Russia Under the Bolshevik Regime: 1919-1924*, Harvill, London, 1994, p401. I have retained his translation since it is consistent with the ideological justification for the use of terror demanded by Lenin.

51. Lenin, *Polnoe sobranie sochinenii*, Vol. 45, Izdatel'stvo politicheskoy literatury, Moscow, 1964, p190.

52. Lenin's wife, N. K. Krupskaya, who saw educational policy as something of a personal portfolio, repeatedly stressed the need in her essays for the "correct" education of children. The main task of education, she believed, was to inculcate the spirit of collectivism:

> We must in the most comprehensive manner exploit all available opportunities ideologically to overcome the petty psychological instinct for private property. From beginning to end schoolchildren must be inculcated with the spirit of collectivism. It is necessary through books to instil the habit in children of relating to every question from the standpoint of the interests of the whole.

See *Izbrannye pedagogicheskie proizvedeniya* (*Selected Pedagogical Works*), Prosveshchenie, Moscow, 1965, pp148-149. She continues: "The best means of education are a correctly adjusted collective life, correctly adjusted work and a comradely, attentive attitude to the children" (p122). Soviet education is ideological indoctrination: "A correctly applied social education must not only help them [children] consciously relate to the phenomena of social life, but also teach them actively to build this life" (p115). Krupskaya stresses the need for "hygiene, personal and social" (p409). In view of the nature of the Soviet state, the emphasis on "social hygiene" has sinister overtones. Education in most Western states seems to have taken Krupskaya's teachings to heart. Individual achievement in our schools is viewed with suspicion, if not open hostility. The methods used to inculcate multiculturalism justify the accusation of ideological indoctrination, with milder forms of "social hygiene" measures, such as ostracism and ridicule, for dissenters.

53. Antony Beevor cites an NKVD [Soviet secret police] report, written in 1945, in which it is noted with some alarm that Soviet soldiers are talking about the obvious comfort of German civilians and forming "politically incorrect conclusions". See Antony Beevor, *Berlin: the Downfall 1945*, Viking, Penguin, London, 2002, p34.

54. In a letter published in *The Times* in 1970, Dr Nina Szamuely, a specialist working on the Oxford Russian Dictionary, wrote that: "[...] the craze for ideologically correct, artificial 'revolutionary' names was extremely widespread in the twenties and early thirties." Girls were given names such as Lenina and Stalina or Russian acronyms such as Revdit—*revolyutsionnoe ditya*—revolutionary child. See *The Last Cuckoo: The Very Best Letters to The Times since 1900*, Unwin Paperbacks, London, 1987, p109.

55. See, for example, Evgeny Dobrenko, *The Making of the State Reader: Social and Aesthetic Contexts of the Reception of Soviet Literature*, trans., Jesse M. Savage, Stanford University Press, Stanford, California, 1997. Lenin laid down the detailed surveillance requirements of librarians in a letter to the People's Commissariat for Enlightenment in 1919. See Lenin, 'V narodnyy kommissariat prosveshcheniya' ('To the People's Commissariat of Enlightenment', 1919), *Sochineniya*, Vol. 28, 4th edition, OGIZ, Moscow 1950, pp429-430.

56. *Kommunisticheskaya partiya sovetskogo soyuza. V rezolyutsiakh i resheniyakh s'ezdov, konferentsii i plenumov TsK* (*The Communist Party of the Soviet Union. In the Resolutions and Decisions of Congresses,. Conferences and Plenums of the Central Committee*), Part II, 1924-1930, Seventh edition, Gosudarstvennoe izdatel'stvo politicheskoy literatury, Moscow, 1954, p14. Hereinafter cited as KPSS.

57. KPSS, 1954, p111.

58. KPSS, 1954, p113.

59. KPSS, 1954, p554.

60. KPSS, 1954, p555.

61. KPSS, 1954, p559.

62. KPSS, 1954, p560.

63. KPSS, 1954, pp560-561. M. I. Frumkin was a Rightist spokesman in the late 1920s. He was executed in 1938. Note the pun in Russian. Bukharin is described as being "right" (*prav*) which also means politically right, the whole point of the attack on him.

64. KPSS, 1954, p561.

65. KPSS, 1954, p561.

66. KPSS, 1954, p562.

67. KPSS, 1954, p563.

68. KPSS, 1954, p565.

[69.] N. S. Khrushchev, 'Sluzhenie narodu—vysokoe prizvanie sovetskikh pis-ateley' ('Serving the people is the lofty vocation of Soviet writers'), *Pravda*, 24th May 1959, p1.

[70.] Khrushchev, *Pravda*, 24th May 1959, p2. "Correctness" was a major theme of Khrushchev's address to the assembled writers. Unnamed, dissent-ing, individual writers were attacked for wavering in the ideological struggle: "Among the writers as a whole there are individuals who would like to attack those 'assault troops' who have entered into the heat of the ideological struggle against revisionists in a more vigorous manner, while asserting correct, party positions. Apparently, a few people would like to present this matter in such a way that it is precisely these comrades who are guilty of everything. But this, of course, is fundamentally incorrect" (p2). Khrushchev talks of the need to combat revisionism: "It is necessary, in my opinion, to help these comrades in the transition from mistaken views to correct, principled positions" (p2). And he cites and develops Gorky's well known expression of hostility to the class enemy: "Aleksei Maksimovich Gorky put it well: 'If the enemy does not surrender, he is destroyed'. This is profoundly correct. That is a class point of view, we have supported and do support it in the assessment of the class struggle ... But there is a correct saying—you don't beat a man when he's down. And, if in the ideological struggle, the enemy surrenders, recognises that he is defeated, and expresses a willingness to assume correct positions, then don't brush him away..." (p2).

[71.] See, for example, Sidney Bloch & Peter Reddaway, *Russia's Political Hospitals: The Abuse of Psychiatry in the Soviet Union*, with a foreword by Vladimir Bukovsky, Victor Gollancz Ltd, London, 1977. Note the following brutal assessment of Soviet psychiatry which confirms the abuses identified by Bloch and Reddaway: "The only way for a patient to get out of the psychiatric prison was to renounce incorrect views and embrace the official line. Again, the healthy psyche was equated with discursiveness, the ability to spout cor-rect verbiage, the eagerness with which one was willing to present ideologi-cally correct precepts as personal convictions. Cited in *Russian Culture at the Crossroads: Paradoxes of Postcommunist Consciousness*, ed., Dmitri N. Shalin, Westview Press, Colorado and Oxford, 1996, p121.

[72.] Two years before the promulgation of the doctrine of socialist realism, Krup-skaya argued for the importance of politically correct reading material and its correct analysis:

> The correctly formulated teaching of literature has massive signifi-cance—now more than ever before. It is necessary only to be able to awaken the children's independence, to teach them collective work in the given area, to organise their independence, to come to their help. (Krupskaya, 1965, p331.)

"[...] the whole programme," she argued, "the whole character of the student's school and external activity, must help his correct approach to works of literature" (Krupskaya, 1965, p329). And again:

> The influence of literature is particularly strong in transitional periods when the social structure is changing, and with it, the old, habitual views on phenomena and the interrelations to people are changing. But not all literature "inflames the heart" and leads the way forward. There also exists a type of literature which pulls one backwards, to the old, which clouds one's vision and disorientates. One must not close one's eyes to this fact. Such literature functions as a kind of poison. Protection from such literature and its influence is necessary. All of this bespeaks the importance of the correct application of the teaching of literature in our school (Krupskaya, 1965, p326).

[73.] Cynthia Ruder, *Making History for Stalin: The Story of the Belomor Canal*, University Press of Florida, Gainsville, 1998, p157. For a detailed discussion of Ruder's book see Frank Ellis, 'The Decline and Fall of History', *Salisbury Review*, Vol. 20, No. 2, 2001, pp28-32.

[74.] Joseph Berger, *Shipwreck of a Generation*, Harvill Press, London, 1971, pp52-53.

[75.] Martin Dewhirst has also made the connection between socialist realism and political correctness: "I would therefore suggest that *pravdivyy* and *pravedvost'* as used in the official definition of Socialist realism mean not so much 'truthful' and 'truthfulness' (when Russians want to insist that some *pravda* really does correspond to the Western concept of truth they talk about *istinnaia pravda*) as *pravednyi* and *pravdenost'* ('righteous' and 'righteousness') and *pravil'nyi* and *pravil'nost'* ('correct' and 'correctness', in other words 'morally and ideologically right' or, as we might say these days, 'politically correct'"'. See 'Soviet Socialist Realism and the Soviet Censorship System' in Hilary Chung, *et al* ed., *In the Party Spirit: Socialist Realism and Literary Practice in the Soviet Union, East Germany and China*, Rodopi, Amsterdam and Atlanta, 1996, p26. The Russian word for government (*pravitel'stvo*) and the verb to govern (*pravit'*) are also etymologically linked to the notion of *pravda*: those who know this "higher truth" are those fit to govern.

[76.] Czesław Miłosz, *The Captive Mind* (1953), trans., Jane Zielonko, Penguin, 1985, p126. Valentin Turchin records what happened to Grigory Pomerants, a Soviet dissident writer: "Someone complained to the Party Bureau about an 'incorrect ideological line' at the seminar, and I was summoned to give an explanation." See Turchin, 1981, p12.

[77.] Andrei Platonov, 'Kotlovan' ('The Foundation Pit', 1929-1930) in *Sobranie sochinenii*, Vol. 2, Informpechat', Moscow, 1998, p332.

[78.] H. C. Chuang, *The Little Red Book and Current Chinese Language*, Studies in Chinese Communist Terminology, No. 13, Centre for Chinese Studies Institute of International Studies, University of California Berkley, California, August 1968, pp7-8.

[79.] Note the changes from the original "Great Proletarian Cultural Revolution" in the 1960s to "Cultural Revolution" in the 1970s and 1980s to, currently, "cultural revolution". Schoenhals, 1992, p109.

[80.] Boris Pasternak, *Dr Zhivago*, Feltrinelli, Milan, 1957, p519.

[81.] Jung Chang, who lived through the cultural revolution, admitted that on hearing of Mao's death she had to hide the lack of "correct emotion". See Jung Chang, *Wild Swans: Three Daughters of China* (1991), Flamingo, Harper/ Collins, 1993, p658. The expectation that every Chinese was supposed to be stricken with grief on hearing of Mao's death has a parallel with the capricious blood-letting inflicted by the Zulu king Chaka on his people after his mother died. Hundreds, possibly thousands, were executed for failing to make appropriate and prolonged displays of grief. See John R. Baker, *Race*, Oxford University Press, New York and London, 1974, pp289-390.

[82.] Jing Lin, *The Red Guards' Path to Violence: Political, Educational and Psychological Factors*, Praeger, Westport, Connecticut, 1991, p40. Lin provides confirmation of the broad definition of Soviet political correctness given above. She notes that: "[...] there is in any given situation just one 'correct line' of policy, all others tend to lead to ruin, and so on" (p.70). Michael Schoenhals's study is a painstaking analysis of the extreme importance attached by Chinese Communist Party theoreticians to the use of correct formulations (*tifa*) and confirms the fundamental approach to language and power shared by both the former Soviet Union and Communist China. Thom in her study of Soviet Newspeak anticipates many of the points made by Schoenhals. See Françoise Thom, *Newspeak: The Language of Soviet Communism*, trans., Ken Connolly, The Claridge Press, London, 1989.

[83.] Lin, 1991, p57.

[84.] Lin, 1991, p79.

[85.] Lin, 1991, p122.

[86.] Lin, 1991, p156.

[87.] Note, for example, the title of Mao's work published in 1957, *On the Correct Handling of Contradictions Among the People*. We are told that the *Talks at the Yenan Forum on Literature and Art* gave artists the "correct orientation". See *Important Documents on the Great Proletarian Cultural Revolution in China*. Foreign Languages Press (FLP), Peking, 1970, p235.

[88.] FLP, 1970, p75.

[89.] FLP, 1970, p65.

[90.] FLP, 1970, p66

[91.] FLP, 1970, p106.

[92.] FLP, 1970, p134.

[93.] FLP, 1970, p230.

[94.] FLP, 1970, p240.

[95.] FLP, 1970, p257.

[96.] FLP, 1970, p274.

[97.] FLP, 1970, p276.

[98.] FLP, 1970, p279.

[99.] *Selected Works of Mao Tsetung*, 1st edn., Vol. 5, Foreign Language Press, Peking, 1977, p405.

[100.] Union Research Service, Issue Nos, 1-26, January-March, Vol. 50, Kowloon, Hong Kong, 1968, p121.

[101.] *Editor's and Writer's Friend* (1984). Cited in Schoenhals, 1992, p76. An example of an incorrect formulation among a majority of Western scholars would be the use of "totalitarian" to refer to the Soviet Union. To quote Martin Malia: "In the introduction to each new monograph, the totalitarian model was ritually excoriated, and the 'T-word' was banished from polite academic discourse, its used viewed as virtual incitement to Cold War hostility towards the 'Evil Empire'. By the onset of *perestroika* in 1985, a pall of political correctness had settled over the field." See Martin Malia, *The Soviet Tragedy: A History of Socialism in Russia, 1917-1991*, The Free Press, New York, 1994, p12.

[102.] *Documents of Chinese Communist Party Central Committee Sept. 1956 - Apr. 1969*, Vol. 1, Union Research Institute, Kowloon, Hong Kong, 1971, p223.

[103.] Schoenhals, 1992, p63.

[104.] *Documents of the Chinese Communist Party*, 1971, p243.

[105.] A Directive of the Chinese Communist Party on the Rectification Campaign (27th April 1957) offers some advice on rectification procedures in which victims are expected to confess to non-existent crimes: "Comradely heart-to-heart talks in the form of conversations, namely exchange of views between individuals, should be used more and large meetings of criticism or 'struggle' should not be held. Criticism should be boldly encouraged when it is done at discussion or group meetings or in the course of individual talks. The principle of 'telling all that you know, and telling it without reservation; blaming not the speaker but heeding what you hear; correcting mistakes if you have committed them and avoiding them if you have not' should be firmly adhered to." See, *Documents of Chinese Communist Party*, 1971, p255.

[106.] Kate Saunders *et al.*, *Eighteen Layers of Hell: Stories from the Chinese Gulag*, with a foreword by Harry Wu, Cassell, London, 1996, p73.

[107.] Saunders, 1996, pvii. In their study of psychiatric abuse in the Soviet Union Bloch and Reddaway considered the possibility of such abuses occurring in other communist states. Of China they noted: "As for China, no reliable evidence of psychiatric abuse is available to us. But the apparently widespread practice of trying to cure mental illness by inculcating Maoism into patients so that they should think 'correctly' arouses the suspicion that psychiatrists may also be involved in the 'thought reform' practised on dissenters in labour camps." See Bloch & Reddaway, 1977, p466. Twenty five years later the evidence for such psychiatric abuse is detailed and abundant.

[108.] Saunders, 1996, p41.

[109.] Union Research Service, 1968, p225.

[110.] See here Paul Hollander, *Political Pilgrims: Travels of Western Intellectuals to the Soviet Union, China and Cuba 1928-1978*, OUP, New York and Oxford, 1981.

[111.] Roger Scruton, *Thinkers of the New Left*, Claridge Press, London, 1985, p7.

[112.] Scruton, 1985, p7.

[113.] Scruton, 1985, p77.

[114.] This is taken from the 1969 revised edition of *The Affluent Society*. In the 1963 edition of Galbraith's book, the underlined text is absent.

[115.] Convinced to the bitter end that the Soviet state could be reformed, Mikhail Gorbachev, the last Soviet leader, was still thinking in outmoded Leninist terms and praising Leninist norms, as the Soviet Union entered its terminal phase: "Most of us adhere to correct political and ideological principles. But there is a substantial distance between a correct stand and its realization." See Mikhail Gorbachev, *Perestroika: New Thinking for Our Country and the World*, Collins, London, 1987, p65. Earlier, Gorbachev writes of the "correctness" of his own policies (p58).

[116.] For a succinct and penetrating discussion of the role of the Frankfurt School in formulating and propagating New Left ideology see Patrick J. Buchanan, *The Death of the West: How Dying Populations and Immigrant Invasions Imperil Our Country and Civilization*, St. Martin's Press, New York, 2002, pp73-96.

[117.] Though, as Etkind points out, the belief that human beings can be remoulded is fundamental to Soviet Marxism: "Man is seen as plastic material which is suitable for creation. He has no natural qualities, he is totally immersed in culture and is formed by the purposeful influences of milieu, society and science. In other words, man's nature is no longer seen as *nature*. It is seen as culture, the result of mankind's efforts or those of its best representatives. Nature-as-culture loses its inherent qualities—primacy, innateness and sense of detachment from others, the fundamental independence of its efforts. What is made by people, can be remade. Man's nature becomes an object of purposeful manipulations." See Alexander Etkind, 'Kul´tura protiv prirody: Psikhologia russkogo moderna' ('Culture against Nature: the psychology of the Russian Modern') *Oktyabr´*, 7, 1993, p184 (emphasis in the original).

[118.] Chuang, 1968, p47.

[119.] I have borrowed Thom's remark about the effect of Marxism-Leninism on language: "Ideology turns the world into language." Thom, 1989, p87.

[120.] Frank Ellis, 'Information, Communication and Control: Towards the New Censorship Paradigm', in *Advances in Sociocybernetics and Human Development, Volume VIII: Evolution of Man and Society in the Age of Accelerating Changes, Potential Benefits, Challenges to Human Development*, George Lasker ed., The International Institute for Advanced Studies, Ontario, Canada, 2000, p57.

[121.] Robert Conquest, *The Great Terror. A Reassessment*, Hutchinson, London, 1990, p131.

[122.] Cited in Henry Beard & Christopher Cerf, eds., *The Official Politically Correct Dictionary & Handbook*, Grafton, Harper/Collins, London. 1992, p97.

[123.] Bear & Cerf, 1992, p87.

[124.] Robert Hughes, *Culture of Complaint: The Fraying of America*, Oxford University Press, New York and Oxford, 1993, p28.

[125.] Burt, 2001, p1901.

[126.] Harry Wu and Carolyn Wakeman. *Bitter Winds: A Memoir of My Years in China's Gulag*, John Wiley & Sons Inc, New York, 1994, p87.

[127.] See Alan Charles Kors, 'Thought Reform 101: The Orwellian Implications of Today's College Orientation', *Reason Magazine*, http://www.reason.com, March 2000.

[128.] The article in which Ray Honeyford drew attention to what was happening in his school was first published in *The Salisbury Review* in 1984. The race riots in Oldham, Burnley and Leeds in 2001 were a direct consequence of trends which Honeyford had earlier identified. The article was reprinted in 2001. 'Education and Race—an Alternative View', *The Salisbury Review*, Vol. 20, No. 1, 2001, pp9-12.

[129.] Robert J. Lifton, *Thought Reform and the Psychology of Totalism: A Study of "Brainwashing" in China*, Victor Gollancz Ltd, London, 1961, p438. Multiculturalists are quite prepared to avail themselves of the same coercive methods used by Mao and the Chinese Communist Party. In a wide-ranging report on multiculturalism in Britain, Bhikhu Parekh, a prominent guru of multiculturalism, cites a respondent who argues that: "People in positions of power *must really believe*, in their hearts and minds, that black and white are equal." See *The Future of Multi-Ethnic Britain: Report of the Commission on the Future of Multi-Ethnic Britain*, Profile Books, London, 2000, p141 (emphasis added). In chapter 20 of the same report we are given the thoughts of an anonymous race bureaucrat: "Training is encouraging people, but we have reached the stage where *people must be told to do it or else*," p284 (emphasis added). For an analysis of this report see Frank Ellis, 'Race, Marxism and the "Deconstruction" of the United Kingdom', *The Journal of Social, Political and Economic Studies*, Vol. 26, No. 4, Winter 2001, pp691-718.

[130.] For a detailed study of academic persecution in the USA and Canada, see Roger Pearson, *Race, Intelligence and Bias in Academe*, Introduction by Hans J. Eysenck, 2nd edition, Scott-Townsend Publishers, Washington, D.C., 1997.

[131.] In a book published in 1993, Richard Lanham, a professor at the University of California, Los Angeles (UCLA), argued that: "Literary study, as by now we all know, takes place very largely in a university environment, and that environment is far more open and democratic than it used to be, and draws upon a student body far more multilingual and multicultural than any of us contemplated even twenty years ago." See Richard A. Lanham, *The Electronic Word: Democracy, Technology and the Arts*, The University of Chicago Press, Chicago and London, 1993, p23. While one can grant the presence of multiculturalism in the university, the idea that this has been accompanied by greater openness is emphatically not the case. Demands to respect "diversity" have all too frequently been used to silence justified criticism of multiculturalism and feminism. Ten years on, things have become much worse on both sides of the Atlantic.

[132.] See Stephen Robinson, 'Heavyweight bout ends in victory for all', *The Daily Telegraph*, 2nd May 2002, p34. Parekh does not go as far as Kennedy but the fact that he writes of "so-called political correctness" reveals an attempt to dismiss it as something of little consequence. See Parekh, 2000, p163.

[133.] To quote Paul Hollander: "The tenacious 'leftism' of Western intellectuals and the continued (or periodically resurgent) hold of (of some version of) Marxism on them was one of the interesting findings of this study. So was the attraction exercised by almost any set of claims, slogans, and terminology vaguely Marxist. As will be further discussed below, Old and New Left were united—despite many differences—in being drawn emotionally to some variety of Marxism or some elements of Marxism." See Hollander, 1981, p22.

[134.] Marred in places by a failure to recognise some fundamental differences between the USA and the two communist superpowers (the former Soviet Union and Communist China), Schoenhals's book, in spite of the author's best efforts to avoid making any parallels with feminism and multiculturalism, is essential reading for understanding the debt owed by Western versions of political correctness to Mao and his successors.

[135.] See Jonathan N. Lipman & Stevan Harrell, eds., *Violence in China: Essays in Culture and Counterculture*, State University of New York Press, 1990.

[136.] Saunders, 1996.

[137.] See Chung *et al*, ed., 1996.

[138.] For example, Bichler, pp30-43, Chung, pxvi, Chung & McClellan, pp1-22, Wallace, pp78-87, Lan, pp88-105, Chung *et al*, ed., 1996.

[139.] Dewhirst, in Chung *et al*, ed., 1996, p26.

[140.] Chung *et al*, ed., 1996, pxvi.

[141.] As in Russell Kirk, *Redeeming the Time*, Intercollegiate Studies Institute, Wilmington Delaware, 1996, pp3-4 and Richard Weaver, *Ideas Have Consequences* (1948), University of Chicago Press, Chicago and London, 1984, p138.

[142.] Thus the camp, the corrective labour camp (*ispravitel′no-trudovoy lager′*), was where the prisoner was dispatched to be "corrected", at least in theory.

[143.] Alexander Solzhenitsyn, *The Gulag Archipelago 1918-1956: An Experiment in Literary Investigation* (1973) Volume 1, trans., Thomas Witney, Harper Collins, 1991, pp173-174.

[144.] In *The Falsification of the Good*, Besançon comments on Orwell's term crimestop: "it [crimestop] includes the ability not to perceive logical errors and not to comprehend the simplest of arguments if they are against *Ingsoc*, and, inversely, to have an aversion to any train of thought capable of leading in an undesirable direction. It is 'protective stupidity'". See Besançon, 1994, p119. Is this an explanation?

[145.] See Sir William Macpherson of Cluny, *The Stephen Lawrence Inquiry: Report of an Inquiry by Sir William Macpherson of Cluny*, CM 4262-I, The Stationery Office, London, 1999. For analysis of this report see Frank Ellis, *The Macpherson Report: "Anti-Racist"Hysteria and the Sovietization of the United Kingdom*, Right Now Press Limited, London, 2001. For a brief discussion of the impact of political correctness on the armed forces see Frank Ellis, 'Political Correctness Attacks the Armed Forces' (Response to the Strategic Defence Review, Part 2), *Freedom Today*, Vol. 24, Issue 1, February/March 1999, p16. Another emerging threat is the race legislation of the European Union, especially the proposal for an EU law to combat racism and xenophobia (*Proposal for a Council Framework Decision on Combating Racism and Xenophobia*, COM (2001) 664, 28.11.2001). For a discussion of this legislation, see Frank Ellis, 'Race Legislation in the European Union', *The Journal of Social, Political and Economic Studies*, volume 27 No 3, Fall, 2002, pp257-269. According to the EU proposal, racism and xenophobia "shall mean the belief in race, colour, descent, religion or belief, national or ethnic origin as a factor determining aversion to individuals or groups" (Article 3, paragraph (a)). One of Britain's law lords, Lord Scott, stated that the definition of xenophobia "would almost certainly cover the distribution of Biggles and probably the Old Testament." Philip Johnston, 'Extradition law may give EU police power of arrest in Britain', *The Daily Telegraph*, 1st November 2002, p10.

[146.] Dyke's remarks were made during the course of an interview on BBC Radio Scotland (7th January 2001).

[147.] See Rod Liddle, 'Why is the BBC so scared of the truth?', *The Spectator*, 10th May 2003, p15.

148. Liddle, 2003, p14.

149. John Grieve, 'The evidence against me is compelling. I am a policeman guilty of racism', *The Daily Telegraph*, 10th May 2000, p15.

150. Macpherson refers with obvious approval to Stokely Carmichael's *Black Power: The Politics of Liberation in America* (1967). See Macpherson, 1999, p23.

151. One white police officer based in London told me that as he left his station at the end of a shift, he was approached by two blacks, a man and a woman, who asked him for directions. The police officer is convinced that he was being "integrity tested" and that the testers were hoping to find some hostility to blacks in his reply.

152. Macpherson's own attitude towards the "diversity" which he insists the police and British society must embrace can be seen in his choice of permanent domicile, deep in the Scottish Highlands, somewhat removed from the multicultural murder and mayhem of London and other cities.

153. John Aspinall, 'Crime Gnawing at our National Values', *The Daily Telegraph*, 4th October 1999, p19. However, given the large numbers of black muggers, this state of denial could not be maintained indefinitely. Even Ian Blair, one of the more politically-correct senior police officers at Scotland Yard, was forced to concede that nearly two-thirds of muggings were carried out by blacks. See Jo Butler, 'Truth about race and muggers, by liberal police chief', *Daily Mail*, 11th October 2002, p37.

154. In the words of another London-based police officer: "People are leaving the force at the very time when crime is soaring in South London, much of it committed by gangs of illegal immigrants from eastern Europe, Africa and Jamaica. So not only are we permanently overstretched, rushing from one incident to another, but also our work is hamstrung by fear of charges of 'racism'. In the past, when I saw an incident on the street, I would have carried out a stop-and-search of potential suspects. But now I think twice, asking myself if it is really worth it. All I'm likely to end up with is a complaint against me and that'll undermine my career." Quoted in Leo McKinstry, 'Capital Crimes', *The Spectator*, 25th November 2000, p28. Nor are adults the sole victims of the Macpherson doctrine. Called a "teletubby" by an Asian pupil, a 10-year old white boy responded with "Paki bastard". The High Court has ruled that the boy can be prosecuted for "racially aggravated assault". Editorial, 'The Trouble with Macpherson', *The Daily Telegraph*, 11th April 2001, p29.

155. Soon after the publication of Agatha Christie's novel in 1939 the title was changed to *Ten Little Indians*, which remains the current title. In the contemporary lexicon of political correctness "Indian" has now been replaced by the politically correct "native Americans" and "little" is also suspect. So we can expect another bout of renaming, with rather amusing consequences, *Ten Verti-*

cally Challenged Native Americans perhaps. This politically correct obsession with renaming follows the Soviet pattern of renaming cities and towns when some senior party official was arrested and became an unperson. For example, after Stalin's death Stalingrad was renamed Volgograd. Nor is it just a case of a change of title. Works deemed "unacceptable" are as likely to be rewritten as brushed aside. Well before the current assertion of the multicultural and feminist agendas, demands were made of the American writer, Ray Bradbury, to change his work. Female readers of *The Martian Chronicles* wanted the author to rewrite the book and include more female characters and roles. Others complained that blacks in the book bore too much of a resemblance to Uncle Tom, some that the work was prejudiced in favour of blacks. In Bradbury's *The Fog Horn* deletions were made before the story was included in a high school reader. An American university refused to put on a production of Bradbury's play *Leviathan 99* because there were no female roles. The dangers of such bowdlerization for the literary enterprise and culture generally are quite clear: "Every short story, slenderized, starved, bluepenciled, leeched and bled white, resembled every other story. Twain read like Poe read like Shakespeare read like Dostoevsky read like—in the finale—Edgar Guest. Every word of more than three syllables had been razored. Every image that demanded so much as one instant's attention—shot dead! [...] The point is obvious. There is more than one way to burn a book. And the world is full of people running about with lit matches." See Coda in Ray Bradbury, *Fahrenheit 451* (1953), Ballantine Books, New York, 1990, pp176-177. In the current climate it would not be too difficult to imagine the works of Russian writers being subjected to the same bowdlerization so as not to offend their English readers in translation. Two contenders would be Vasiliy Grossman and Alexander Solzhenitsyn. In *Everything Flows* Grossman makes no concessions to contemporary fashions on homosexual rights, describing the physical and moral debasement inflicted by lesbians on other women in the camps:

> In the camps women forced other women to live in unnatural cohabitation. In the women's prison camps ridiculous characters came into being, lesbians, with hoarse voices and a bold gait, who, aping the manners of men, wore their trousers tucked into soldiers' boots. And alongside them stood these lost, pitiful creatures—their bitches. (See Grossman, 1974, pp98-99.)

In *Cancer Ward*, Solzhenitsyn describes in scathing terms the complete incompetence of a doctor, drawn from one of the Soviet ethnic minorities, who, as part of the Soviet version of equal opportunities, has been promoted way beyond his limited abilities and so represents a very real threat to the well-being of hospital patients:

Lev Leonidovich could see curly-haired Halmuhamedov particularly well from where he sat. He looked like an illustration from the travels of Captain Cook, a savage straight out of the jungle. His hair was a dense mat, his bronzed face was spotted with jet-carbon blackheads, his ferociously gleeful smile revealed a large set of white teeth—there was only one thing missing: a ring through his nose. Of course it was not his appearance that mattered, or the neatly inscribed certificate he had received from medical college, it was that he could not carry out a single operation without bungling it. Lev Leonidovich had let him operate a couple of times, but now swore he would never let him do it again. To sack him, however, was equally out of the question. That would be called undermining the policy of training native person-nel. So the man had now spent more than three years writing case histories, only the simple ones of course. He went on doctors' rounds and looked important, visited the dressings room and did night-duty (during which he slept). Lately he'd even started drawing his salary on a time-and-a-half basis, even though he left the hospital at the end of the working day. See Alexander Solzhenitsyn, *Cancer Ward*, Penguin, Harmondsworth, 1971, p381.

Having smashed a fair few Soviet taboos in their time, Grossman and Solzhen-itsyn, two of Russia's greatest writers, reject two articles of faith of the left: any notion of homosexual rights; and that which believes in rewarding an individual because of his racial origins not because of his abilities.

[156.] Cited in *Conquest*, 1990, p112.

[157.] Vladimir Makanin, *Baize-Covered Table with Decanter* (1993) trans., Arch Tait, Readers International, London, 1995, p46.

References and further reading

Apter, David., ed. *Ideology and Discontent*, The Free Press, New York and London, 1964.

Arendt, Hannah. *The Origins of Totalitarianism* (1961), Harcourt Brace Jovanovich, New York and London, 1973.

Aspinall, John. Letters, 'Crime Gnawing at our National Values', *The Daily Telegraph*, 4th October 1999, p19.

Baker, John R. *Race*, Oxford University Press, New York and London, 1974.

Beard, Henry & Cerf, Christopher, eds. *The Official Politically Correct Dictionary & Handbook*, Grafton, Harper/Collins, London, 1992.

Beevor, Antony. *Berlin: the Downfall 1945*, Viking, Penguin, London, 2002.

Beglov, Spartak I. *Vneshnepoliticheskaya propaganda: Ocherk teorii i praktiki (Foreign Policy Propaganda: An Essay in Theory and Practice)*, Vneshnyaya shkola, Moscow, 1984.

Berger, Joseph. *Shipwreck of a Generation*, Harvill Press, London, 1971.

Besançon, Alain. *The Falsification of the Good: Soloviev and Orwell*, trans., Matthew Screech, The Claridge Press, London, 1994.

Bloch, Sidney & Reddaway, Peter. *Russia's Political Hospitals: The Abuse of Psychiatry in the Soviet Union*, with a foreword by

Vladimir Bukovsky, Victor Gollancz Ltd, London, 1977.

Bradbury, Ray. *Fahrenheit 451* (1953), Ballantine Books, New York, 1990.

Buchanan, Patrick J. *The Death of the West: How Dying Populations and Immigrant Invasions Imperil Our Country and Civilization*, St. Martin's Press, New York, 2002.

Burt, Richard. 'Political Correctness', in Derek Jones, ed., *Censorship: A World Encyclopedia*, Vol. 3, Fitzroy Dearborn Publishers, London, 2001.

Butler, Jo, 'Truth about race and muggers, by liberal police chief', *Daily Mail*, 11th October 2002, p37.

Chang, Jung. *Wild Swans: Three Daughters of China* (1991), Flamingo, Harper/Collins, 1993.

Chuang, H. C. *The Little Red Book and Current Chinese Language*, Studies in Chinese Communist Terminology, No. 13, Centre for Chinese Studies Institute of International Studies, University of California Berkley, California, August 1968.

Chung, Hilary *et al* ed. *In the Party Spirit: Socialist Realism and Literary Practice in the Soviet Union, East Germany and China*, Rodopi, Amsterdam and Atlanta, 1996.

The Concise Oxford Russian Dictionary, Revised edition, Oxford University Press, Oxford, 1998.

Conquest, Robert. *The Great Terror: A Reassessment*, Hutchinson, London, 1990.

Counts, G. S & Lodge, N. *The Country of the Blind: The Soviet System of Mind Control*, Boston: Houghton Mifflin Co., 1949.

Dobrenko, Evgeny. *The Making of the State Reader: Social and Aesthetic Contexts of the Reception of Soviet Literature*, trans., Jesse M. Savage, Stanford University Press, Stanford, California, 1997.

Documents of Chinese Communist Party Central Committee Sept. 1956 - Apr. 1969, Vol. 1, Union Research Institute, Kowloon, Hong Kong, 1971.

Editorial, 'The Trouble with Macpherson', *The Daily Telegraph*, 11th April 2001, p29.

Ellis, Frank. 'Political Correctness Attacks the Armed Forces'

(Response to the Strategic Defence Review, Part 2), *Freedom Today*, Vol. 24, Issue 1, February/March 1999, p16.

'From Marx to MacPherson', *Freedom Today*, Vol. 25, Issue 2, April/May 2000, pp16-17.

'Information, Communication and Control: Towards the New Censorship Paradigm', in *Advances in Sociocybernetics and Human Development, Volume VIII: Evolution of Man and Society in the Age of Accelerating Changes, Potential Benefits, Challenges to Human Development*, George Lasker ed., The International Institute for Advanced Studies, Ontario, Canada, 2000, pp55-60.

'The Decline and Fall of History', *Salisbury Review*, Vol. 20, No. 2, 2001, pp28-32.

The Macpherson Report: 'Anti-Racist' Hysteria and the Sovietization of the United Kingdom, Right Now Press Limited, London, 2001.

'Race, Marxism and the "Deconstruction" of the United Kingdom', *The Journal of Social, Political and Economic Studies*, Vol. 26, No. 4, Winter 2001, pp691-718.

'Race Legislation in the European Union', *The Journal of Social, Political and Economic Studies*, Vol. 27 No. 3, Fall, 2002, pp257-269.

Etkind, Alexander. 'Kul'tura protiv prirody: Psikhologia russkogo moderna' ('Culture against Nature: the psychology of the Russian Modern') *Oktyabr'*, 7, 1993, pp168-192.

Francis, Samuel. *Thinkers of Our Time: James Burnham* (1984), 2nd edition, The Claridge Press, London, 1999.

Galbraith, J. K. *The Affluent Society* (1958), Penguin Books, Harmondsworth, Middlesex, 1963.

Goldberg, Bernard. *Bias: A CBS Insider Exposes How the Media Distort the News*, Regnery Publishing Inc., Washington D.C., 2002.

Gorbachev, Mikhail. *Perestroika: New Thinking for Our Country and the World*, Collins, London, 1987.

Grieve, John. 'The evidence against me is compelling. I am a policeman guilty of racism', *The Daily Telegraph*, 10th May 2000, p15.

Grossman, Vasili. *Vse Techet* (*Everything Flows*), 2nd edition, Possev-Verlag, Frankfurt/Main, Germany, 1974.

Heller, Mikhail. *Cogs in the Soviet Wheel: The Formation of Soviet Man*, trans., David Floyd, Collins, London, 1988.

Hollander, Gayle Durham. *Soviet Political Indoctrination: Developments in Mass Media Since Stalin*, Praeger Publishers, New York and London, 1973.

Hollander, Paul. *Political Pilgrims: Travels of Western Intellectuals to the Soviet Union, China and Cuba 1928-1978*, OUP, New York and Oxford, 1981.

Honeyford, Ray. 'Education and Race - An Alternative View', *The Salisbury Review*, Vol. 20, No. 1, 2001, pp9-12.

Horsfield, Charlotte, 'Snake in the Grass', review of Aidan Rankin, *The Politics of the Forked Tongue*, in *The Salisbury Review*, Vol. 21, No. 3, Spring 2003, pp53-54.

Hughes, Robert. *Culture of Complaint: The Fraying of America*, Oxford University Press, New York and Oxford, 1993.

Important Documents on the Great Proletarian Cultural Revolution in China. Foreign Languages Press, Peking, 1970.

Johnston, Philip. 'Extradition law may give EU police power of arrest in Britain', *The Daily Telegraph*, 1st November 2002, p10.

Khrushchev, N. S. 'Sluzhenie narodu - vysokoe prizvanie sovetskikh pisateley' ('Serving the people is the lofty vocation of Soviet writers'), *Pravda*, 24th May 1959, pp1-3.

Kirk, Russell. *Enemies of the Permanent Things: Observations of Abnormity in Literature and Politics*, Sherwood Sugden & Company, Peru, Illinois, 1984.

Redeeming the Time, Intercollegiate Studies Institute, Wilmington Delaware, 1996.

Kommunisticheskaya partiya sovetskogo soyuza. V rezolyutsiakh i resheniyakh s'ezdov, konferentsii i plenumov TsK (*The Communist Party of the Soviet Union. In the Resolutions and Decisions of Congresses, Conferences and Plenums of the Central Committee*), Part II, 1924-1930, Seventh edition, Gosudarstvennoe izdatel'stvo politicheskoy literatury, Moscow, 1954.

Kors, Alan Charles. 'Thought Reform 101: The Orwellian Implications of Today's College Orientation', *Reason Magazine*, http://www.reason.com, March 2000.

Krupskaya, N. K. *Izbrannye pedagogicheskie proizvedeniya* (*Selected Pedagogical Works*), Prosveshchenie, Moscow, 1965.

Kunitsyn, Georgii. *V. I. Lenin o partiinosti i svobode pechati* (*V. I. Lenin on Party Spirit and the Freedom of the Press*) Izdatel'stvo politicheskoy literatury, Moscow, 1971.

Lanham, Richard A. *The Electronic Word: Democracy, Technology and the Arts*, The University of Chicago Press, Chicago and London, 1993.

The Last Cuckoo: The Very Best Letters to The Times since 1900, Unwin Paperbacks, London, 1987.

Lenin, V. I. 'S chego nachat'?' ('How to Begin?', 1901), *Sochineniya*, Vol. 5, 4th edition, OGIZ, Moscow, 1946, pp5-12.

Chto delat'? (*What is to be Done?*, 1902), *Sochineniya*, Vol. 5, 4th edition, OGIZ, Moscow, 1946, pp319-492.

'Partiynaya organisatsiya i partiynaya literatura' ('Party Organisation and Party Literature', 1905) *Sochineniya*, Vol. 10, 4th edition, OGIZ, Moscow, 1947, pp26-31.

'Sotsialisticheskaya partiya i bespartiinaya revolyutsionnost' ('The Socialist Party and the Revolutionary Ethos of the Non-Party Faction', 1905), *Sochineniya*, Vol. 10, 4th edition, OGIZ, Moscow, 1947, pp57-64

"Svoboda kritiki i edinstvo deystvii', ('Freedom of Criticism and Unity of Action', 1906), *Sochineniya*, Vol. 10, 4th edition, OGIZ, Moscow, 1947, pp408-409.

'Plokhie sovety' ('Bad Advice', 1906), *Sochineniya*, Vol. 10, 4th edition, OGIZ, Moscow, 1947, pp410-414.

'Kadety, trudoviki, i rabochaya partiya' ('The Kadets, the workers and the workers' party', 1906), *Sochineniya*, Vol. 10, 4th edition, OGIZ, Moscow, 1947, pp420-424.

'Kak rassuzhdaet t. Plekhanov o taktike sotsial-demokratii'('How Comrade Plekhanov thinks concerning the tactics of Social Democracy', 1906), *Sochineniya*, Vol. 10, 4th edition, OGIZ,

Moscow, 1947, pp425-446.

'Proletarskaya revolyutsiya i renegat Kautskii' ('The Proletarian Revolution and the Renegade Kautsky', 1918), *Sochineniya*, Vol. 28, 4th edition, OGIZ, Moscow, 1950, pp207-302.

'V narodnyy kommissariat prosveshcheniya' ('To the People's Commissariat of Enlightenment', 1919), *Sochineniya*, Vol. 28, 4th edition, OGIZ, Moscow, 1950, pp429-430.

Polnoe sobranie sochinenii, Vol. 45, Izdatel'stvo politicheskoy literatury, Moscow, 1964.

Liddle, Rod. 'Why is the BBC so scared of the truth?', *The Spectator*, 10th May 2003, pp14-15.

Lifton, Robert, J. *Thought Reform and the Psychology of Totalism: A Study of "Brainwashing" in China*, Victor Gollancz Ltd, London, 1961.

Lin, Jing. *The Red Guards' Path to Violence: Political, Educational and Psychological Factors*, Praeger, Westport, Connecticut, 1991.

Lipman, Jonathan N & Harrell, Stevan, eds. *Violence in China: Essays in Culture and Counterculture*, State University of New York Press, 1990.

Macpherson, Sir William of Cluny. *The Stephen Lawrence Inquiry: Report of an Inquiry by Sir William Macpherson of Cluny*, CM 4262-I, The Stationery Office, London, 1999.

Makanin, Vladimir. *Baize-Covered Table with Decanter* (1993), trans., Arch Tait, Readers International, London, 1995.

Malaya Sovetskaya Entsiklopediya (*The Small Soviet Encyclopedia*), Vol. 7, 3rd edn, Gosudarstvennoe nauchnoe izdatel'stvo, Moscow, 1959.

Malia, Martin. *The Soviet Tragedy: A History of Socialism in Russia, 1917-1991*, The Free Press, New York, 1994.

McKinstry, Leo. 'Capital Crimes', *The Spectator*, 25th November 2000, pp28-29.

Medvedev, Zhores. *The Rise and Fall of T. D. Lysenko*, trans., Michael Lerner, Columbia University Press, New York & London, 1969.

Mi□osz, Czes□aw. *The Captive Mind* (1953), trans., Jane Zielonko, Penguin, 1985.

Murphey, Dwight D., 'Conceptual Issues in Prohibiting "Hate Speech"', in *The Mankind Quarterly*, Vol. XLIII, No. 3, Spring 2003, pp335-352.

Parekh, Bhikhu. *The Future of Multi-Ethnic Britain: Report of the Commission on the Future of Multi-Ethnic Britain*, Profile Books, London, 2000.

Pasternak, Boris. *Dr Zhivago*, Feltrinelli, Milan, 1957.

Pearson, Roger. *Race, Intelligence and Bias in Academe*, Introduction by Hans J. Eysenck, 2nd edition, Scott-Townsend Publishers, Washington, D.C., 1997.

Pipes, Richard. *Russia Under the Bolshevik Regime: 1919-1924*, Harvill, London, 1994.

Platonov, Andrei. 'Kotlovan' ('The Foundation Pit', 1929-1930) in *Sobranie sochinenii*, Vol. 2, 'Informpechat', Moscow, 1998.

Rankin, Aidan. *The Politics of the Forked Tongue: Authoritarian Liberlism*, New European Publications, London, 2002.

Resheniya partii i pravitel'stva po khozyaystvennym voprosam (*Decisions of the Party and Government on Economic Questions*) Vol. 1, 1917-1928, Izdatel'stvo politicheskoy literatury, Moscow, 1967.

Robinson, Stephen. 'Heavyweight bout ends in victory for all', *The Daily Telegraph*, 2nd May 2002, p34.

Roxburgh, Angus. *Pravda: Inside the Soviet News Machine*, Victor Gollancz Ltd, London, 1987.

Ruder, Cynthia. *Making History for Stalin: The Story of the Belomor Canal*, University Press of Florida, Gainsville, 1998.

Saunders, Kate *et al*. *Eighteen Layers of Hell: Stories from the Chinese Gulag*, with a foreword by Harry Wu, Cassell, London, 1996.

Schoenhals, Michael. *Doing Things with Words in Chinese Politics*, Chinese Research Monograph Series, Institute of East Asian Studies, University of California, Berkeley, 1992.

Schram, Stuart R. *The Political Thought of Mao Tse-Tung*, Pall Mall Press, London and Dunmow, 1963.

Scruton, Roger. *Thinkers of the New Left*, Claridge Press, London, 1985.

Selected Works of Mao Tsetung, 1st edn, Vol. 5, Foreign Languages Press, Peking, 1977.

Shalin, Dmitri., ed. *Russian Culture at the Crossroads: Paradoxes of Postcommunist Consciousness*, Westview Press, Colorado and Oxford, 1996.

Slovar' russkogo yazyka (*Dictionary of the Russian Language*), 18th edition, Russkii yazyk, Moscow, 1987.

Solzhenitsyn, Alexander. *Cancer Ward*, Penguin, Harmondsworth, 1971.

August 1914 The Red Wheel 1: A Narrative in Discrete Periods of Time, trans., H. T. Willets, Penguin, 1990.

The Gulag Archipelago 1918-1956: An Experiment in Literary Investigation (1973) Vol. 1, trans., Thomas Witney, Harper Collins, 1991.

Stein, Harry. *How I Accidentally Joined the Vast Right-Wing Conspiracy (and Found Inner Peace)*, Delacorte Press, 2000.

Thom, Françoise. *Newspeak: The Language of Soviet Communism*, trans., Ken Connolly, The Claridge Press, London, 1989.

Thurston, Anne, F. *Enemies of the People: The Ordeal of the Intellectuals in China's Great Cultural Revolution*, Harvard University Press, Cambridge, Massachusetts, 1988.

Tolstaya, Tat'yana. 'Politicheskaya korrektnost'' ('Political Correctness'), *Sestry*, Podkova, Moscow, 1998, pp106-138.

Turchin, Valentin. *The Inertia of Fear and the Scientific Worldview*, trans., Guy Daniels, Martin Robertson & Company Ltd, Oxford, 1981.

Union Research Service, Issue Nos, 1-26, January-March, Vol. 50, Kowloon, Hong Kong, 1968.

Vazsonyi, Balint. *America's 30 Years War. Who Is Winning?*, Regnery Publishing Inc., Washington D.C., 1998.

Weaver, Richard. *Ideas Have Consequences* (1948), University of Chicago Press, Chicago and London, 1984.

Wu, Harry and Carolyn Wakeman. *Bitter Winds: A Memoir of My Years in China's Gulag*, John Wiley & Sons Inc, New York, 1994.

Index

A

B

G

H

I

J

K